Level 2 Diploma for IT Users
for City & Guilds

Using the Internet

Level

2

Tina Lawton

Endorsed by

City&
Guilds

www.heinemann.co.uk
✓ Free online support
✓ Useful weblinks
✓ 24 hour online ordering

01865 888058

Heinemann
Inspiring generations

Heinemann Educational Publishers
Halley Court, Jordan Hill, Oxford OX2 8EJ
Part of Harcourt Education

Heinemann is the registered trademark of
Harcourt Education Limited

First published 2003

08   07   06   05   04   03
10   9   8   7   6   5   4   3   2   1

British Library Cataloguing in Publication Data is available
from the British Library on request.

ISBN 0 435 46282 2

Publisher's note
The materials in this Work have been developed by Harcourt Education and the
content and the accuracy are the sole responsibility of Harcourt Education. The City
and Guilds of London Institute accepts no liability howsoever in respect of any
breach of the intellectual property rights of any third party howsoever occasioned or
damage to the third party's property or person as a result of the use of this Work.

The City & Guilds name and logo are the registered trade marks of the City and
Guilds of London Institute and are used under licence.

Typeset by Techset Ltd, Gateshead

Printed in the UK by Thomson Litho Ltd. Glasgow

Acknowledgements
My grateful thanks to: Stuart for giving up a Friday night to be my online 'contact';
Anna and Keith, as ever, for their constant support and encouragement; Paul Hafren,
Principal of Warrington Collegiate Institute, for allowing me to use the college's
virtual learning environment in this book; Franny, who introduced me to the
exciting world that VLEs could open for our students; and last, but by no means
least, Pen, Anna and Alex, who seem to have unfailing patience, humour and faith!

The publishers wish to acknowledge the use of screenshots from the Microsoft
Corporation and to thank the following for permission to reproduce screenshots:
Adobe product screenshots are reprinted with permission from Adobe Systems
Incorporated, pages 53, 54; BBC, pages 3, 76; Google, pages 46, 47; Macromedia, Inc.
page 21; JC Matt Software, page 141; RealNetworks, page 9; Winzip Computing Inc.,
pages 31, 32, 33, 34, 35, 36; Zone Labs Inc., page 128.

The publishers have made every effort to contact holders of material reproduced in
this book. Any omissions will be rectified in subsequent printings if notice is given to
the publishers.

Contents

Introduction

City & Guilds e-Quals is an exciting new range of IT qualifications developed with leading industry experts. These comprehensive, progressive awards cover everything from getting to grips with basic IT to gaining the latest professional skills.

The range consists of both User and Practitioner qualifications. User qualifications (Levels 1–3) are ideal for those who use IT as part of their job or in life generally, while Practitioner qualifications (Levels 2–3) have been developed for those who need to boost their professional skills in, for example, networking or software development.

e-Quals boasts online testing and a dedicated website with news and support materials and web-based training. The qualifications reflect industry standards and meet the requirements of the National Qualifications Framework.

With e-Quals you will not only develop your expertise, you will gain a qualification that is recognised by employers all over the world.

This unit is about using the Internet – learning the skills and techniques to make your surfing, searching and communicating more productive and pleasurable. So much information is out there that it can be difficult to find what you want when you need it, and, having found it, how to use it!

The Internet has changed the way we do business, how we communicate and where we seek information on just about any topic under the sun. There can't be many areas of life that have not been touched in some way by this vast web of information and data, and acquiring the skills to use it well and wisely is worth the time it takes to learn them. Working through the sections, you will be able to find out about a wide range of skills, techniques and Internet-related topics, from archiving to aliases, connecting to conferencing, and viruses to VLEs. You will be able to find out how to make sure you and your computer remain safe while you surf.

Throughout this unit there are challenges to test your knowledge and opportunities to 'try it out' for yourself. At the end of the book there are assignments for you to use as practice to make sure you're absolutely ready to pass the real thing.

Although the book covers the syllabus for the City & Guilds IT User Level 2 Diploma Unit 025, it would be just as helpful for anyone wanting to learn a bit more about using the Internet.

In order to give detailed methods for each task it is necessary to refer to a specific operating system, e-mail software and an internet browser, though the City & Guilds unit is not specific and can be completed using any operating system, e-mail software and internet browser. This book refers to Microsoft Windows ME, Microsoft Outlook Express (e-mail software) and Microsoft Internet Explorer (internet browser).

Section 1 | Setting up your connection

Introduction: A global network

Figure 1.1 A global network

The Internet is a global network of computers in many countries linked together to share information and data. Set up more than thirty years ago, when American scientists created a Net to join their computers together during the period of the Cold War, it has developed over the years to become a sophisticated means of transporting files, images, sound and video clips, as well as sending messages almost instantly across the world using e-mail (electronic mail). To connect to this network, you will need:

- A computer
- A phone line or cable connection
- A modem
- An ISP
- Software, e.g. a web browser, e-mail program, connection software.

Hardware for connecting to the Internet

In most cases this will be a PC (Personal Computer) using Windows Operating System (Windows 98 is really the minimum) or an Apple Mac using the Mac Operating System. To connect to the Net you don't need the latest and fastest processor. A Pentium 200 MHz processor with 32 MB of memory would cope with straightforward Internet surfing, although by current standards this would be a very old specification as modern machines will have over 1 GHz of processing power and more than 256 MB of RAM. You will need a sound card and speakers if you plan to listen to music files or Internet radio, and a good graphics card and plenty of RAM (Random Access Memory) if you want to watch video clips or play online games on your computer. If you plan to use broadband technologies to connect to the Net you may need a more modern computer, equipped with a USB (Universal Serial Bus) port.

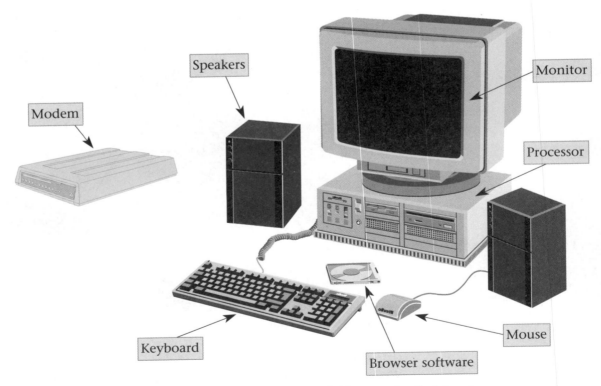

Figure 1.2 The hardware and software needed for accessing the Internet

The phone line or cable connection

Connection to the Net can be through your **phone line** (sometimes called 'narrowband'), an **ISDN** or **Home Highway** digital connection, a **leased line** or, using newer technology, through a **broadband** connection. Bandwidth is a measure of how much data passes between two points over a given connection, so the greater the bandwidth, the greater the number of kilobits (a **bit** is the smallest unit of data) that can be transferred per second. Broadband, as the name suggests, is able to carry considerably more data per second than the conventional phone line.

Using the traditional phone line restricts the speed of data transfer to a maximum of 56 Kbps (Kilobits per second), which can mean a long wait for large files or graphics to download onto your computer. A broadband connection, on the other hand, can download data at speeds up to 512 Kbps and, as technology develops, is getting faster all the time. Such a fast connection would mean that you could download a 50 MB file in less than 15 minutes – many times quicker than a phone line. The time taken for files to download or for web pages to appear on your screen can determine the cost of surfing the Net. If you pay for the call cost when you are online, this can soon mount up to a large bill! With broadband connections, not only is it an 'always on' connection (you don't need to dial your ISP – you have a permanent connection to the Net), but you don't pay for time online as you are usually charged a monthly fee by your ISP.

ISDN (Integrated Services Digital Network) and Home Highway

These provide alternatives to a simple connection to your phone line and consist of digital telephone lines giving you two separate 64 Kbps channels that can be linked together for connection speeds of 128 Kbps. They are both generally available, even if you live in remote areas. Your computer is connected to a special box which is installed in your home.

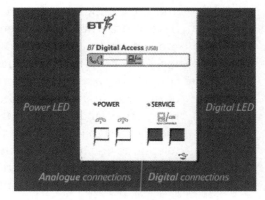

Figure 1.3 A digital access connection

Leased line

Large organisations, such as universities and businesses, often use this extremely fast, direct connection to the Internet by connecting their networks to a special phone line, leased from the phone company. The connection to the Internet is permanent and data is transferred very quickly without the need to dial an ISP's computer. A leased line will be expensive and not usually used by the home surfer.

Broadband

There are three main types of broadband connection available: **ADSL (Asymmetric Digital Subscriber Line)**, **cable** and **satellite**.

ADSL

This is currently the most common form of broadband connection, which requires an upgrade to your phone line and computer system to receive fast Internet access via your phone line. However, you can only use this form of connection if your local telephone exchange has been upgraded to carry ADSL.

Cable

Cable access is provided by some ISPs and uses the same high quality cabling which can pipe TV services into your home, to deliver high-speed Internet access.

Satellite

This technology is expensive and still being developed. It may be some time before it becomes cheap enough and available for the home user.

The modem

This is the interface between your computer and the phone or cable connection to the Internet. The computer produces digital data (0s and 1s); your traditional telephone line only understands analogue signals (waves); the modem **mo**dulates and **dem**odulates the signal so the telephone system and the computer can exchange information. Most modern computers will have an internal V90 modem, although a similar specification external modem can be connected to your machine. With an ADSL broadband connection, a specially adapted version of the 56 K modem is required. This is an external modem, which translates the digital signal sent down your telephone line into fast Internet access. Similar technology is used to connect your computer, via a cable modem, to your cable Internet access provider.

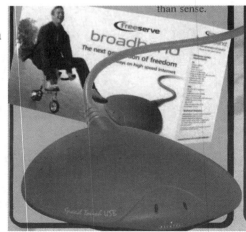

Figure 1.4 A modem

The type and speed of your connection will determine the time it takes for files to be downloaded and for web pages to load. The quicker the speed of data transfer, the less time it will take. If you have a traditional telephone link to your ISP, this can translate into cost if you pay charges for the period you are connected to the Internet.

With a broadband connection, streaming sound and video are of a much higher quality. Broadcasts over the Internet are often **streamed**, so rather than downloading a whole file before starting to watch or listen, your computer will receive a constant flow of data to keep the sound or pictures continuous. With a 56 K modem and a conventional telephone connection you may often find that video or sound broadcasts are jerky and interrupted as the data doesn't reach the computer as quickly as needed.

Most Internet users who connect via their land line can't use their phone to make and receive calls at the same time as surfing. Connecting to the Internet is the same as making a phone call, and anyone calling you will get an engaged tone. An ISDN or ADSL connection will allow you to surf the Net and make and receive calls too.

The Internet is often called the Information Superhighway, and much like our busy roads at rush hour, a large number of people connecting to the Internet and your ISP's servers can slow down the rate of data transfer to a crawl. This can be very noticeable with a traditional phone connection and speeds of transfer at these times can seem very slow indeed. You can check the speed of connection when you are online by double clicking on the connected icon on the taskbar. Even with the newer technologies of ADSL and cable, the rate of data transfer can be affected if all the users sharing your main Internet link start to download large files at the same time.

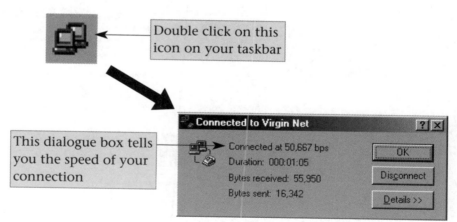

Figure 1.5 Connection speed

The ISP

The **ISP (Internet Service Provider)** is your gateway to the Internet. You can access all the vast store of information on the Internet, including the millions of web pages which make up the World Wide Web, through this gateway. ISPs will also provide other services, such as e-mail, which can keep you in touch with colleagues, friends and family.

Information

The Internet and the World Wide Web (or Web as it is usually called) are terms which are used interchangeably, but they are not the same. The Internet is the underlying structure of connected computers, whereas the Web is a software application that sits on top of the communication hardware and software that is the Internet.

Choosing your ISP can be a confusing process as there are over 200 different providers to choose from. An **Online Service**, such as AOL (America Online), provides a members-only service which will give access to a range of services such as discussion forums, information and shopping, as well as the Internet. An **Internet Service Provider**, such as Freeserve, will

provide access to the Internet. An ISP will have a network connected to other parts of the Internet which you can access by connecting to their servers through your phone line. An ISP provides other functions apart from Internet access:

- Storing messages sent to you for collection when you log on.
- Providing web space if you want to have your own web site.
- Subscribers can join chat rooms, access information services and take advantage of special offers.
- E-mail facilities to send and receive messages.
- Offering help and support if something goes wrong.

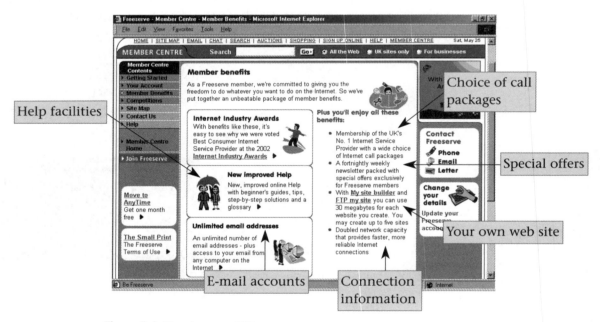

Figure 1.6 Choosing your ISP

A checklist for choosing your ISP

Is it easy to install?

Most ISPs will provide the software you need to connect to the Internet which will be pre-configured with all the settings needed by your computer to make sure that connecting is as straightforward as possible.

Is it reliable?

An ISP should have sufficient capacity to cope with a large number of subscribers. It can be very frustrating to suddenly find you've been disconnected or, even worse, that you can't get connected at all and have to dial into your ISP's server many times before your can send your e-mail messages or search the Net for the information you need.

What's the cost?

- **Free ISPs** If you are only using the Internet for a few hours a month, it may be cheaper to just pay for the time you spend online in phone charges. With this option you don't pay a monthly subscription charge and the services offered can be accessed for free.
- **Unmetered ISPs** If you spend more than about 20 hours per month, it may be that an unmetered ISP would be better value. An unmetered ISP will charge a monthly fee which will allow you to 'surf' the Net for no extra charge, although there may be some conditions to your access, such as evenings and weekends only, or a cut-off time of 2–3 hours to ensure that you don't stay connected for long periods of time.
- **Using broadband** After paying for the specially adapted modem to connect using this fast technology, and an activation charge to BT for converting your phone line into an ADSL-enabled broadband connection, you will still need to pay your ISP a monthly fee, although this will give you unlimited, 'always on' access to the Internet. Most ISPs will support a broadband connection, but it would be wise to check before choosing your provider.

> **BTopenworld Broadband**
>
> • high speed (500k) internet access
> • 'always on' - no dial up, no time restrictions
> • surf and talk at the same time

Figure 1.7 Broadband connection

What if something goes wrong?

If you find that you have a problem with your Internet connection it may be time to call the ISP's technical support. The charge for this can vary from the cost of a local call to £1 a minute or more. If you are using a broadband connection you will need to consider the quality and price of its technical support as it can be quite a complicated procedure for a beginner and you may find that you need some advice.

What other services are offered?

- **E-mail addresses** ISPs offer anything from one address to unlimited addresses, so if you and your family want separate e-mail addresses this might be an important consideration.

> **Unlimited email addresses**
>
> An unlimited number of email addresses - plus access to your email from any computer on the Internet ▶

Figure 1.8 You can have access to more than one e-mail address

- **Web space** Most ISPs will allow you to build your own web pages and upload them to their server. There can be quite large differences in the amount of web space they will provide – anything from 5 MB to unlimited space. If you plan to build a large web site, you might need to look for an ISP which will allow you more than 15 MB.
- **Other services** These can vary from providing content filtering software, if you are worried about keeping children safe when using the Internet, to special deals on goods and services.

Which ISP is the best?

Before choosing your ISP, some research would give you many of the answers to these questions. Most computer magazines have regular reviews of ISPs, giving details of charges and services offered. Visiting the web sites of ISPs will also provide some information to help you to decide which one you prefer. It's always worth asking friends and family if they would recommend an ISP – quite often they will give a practical view of issues such as connecting at the first attempt, the frequency that the line is dropped, value for money.

Software for connecting to the Internet

The web browser

To complete your connection you will need to load the software which translates the information on the Net into documents you can see on screen – a web browser. Most web browsers will have other functions too, such as access to e-mail, downloading files and allowing you to search for and print out information. The majority of ISPs will provide a CD-ROM with the browser software already configured to make setting up the connection a straightforward task. **Microsoft Internet Explorer** and **Netscape Navigator** are two of the most popular browsers, although there are other less well known browsers, such as Opera, NeoPlanet, CrystalPort Browser. Most of these browsers will have slightly different interfaces and functions, but they will all allow you to access the Net. The instructions and illustrations in this book use Internet Explorer, but many of the features are common to most of the browsers.

What is a browser?

A browser is simply a program loaded onto your computer, much like any other program you may use, enabling it to communicate with the web servers on the Internet. Web pages are produced using a programming language called **HTML** (HyperText Markup Language) and browsers need to be able to read HTML documents and text, much as you may use Word to read your word processed documents. As each version of a browser is developed, it will provide more functions, such as being able to play videos, sound files and even 3D imaging. Currently, Internet Explorer Version 6 is the latest release of Microsoft's browser and Version 7 of Netscape Navigator has been developed. To get the best from your surfing experience it is worth checking web sites regularly to see if an updated browser has been released. Internet Explorer comes included in the Windows Operating System, although it can be downloaded free from the Microsoft web site http:// www.microsoft.com. Netscape Navigator can also be downloaded from the Net and installed on your computer from the Netscape web site at http:// home.netscape.com.

> ## Information
>
> To see which version of Internet Explorer you have installed on your computer, click on the **Help** button on the toolbar and select the **About Internet Explorer** option from the menu. You will be able to see the version number in the dialogue box which appears.

Plug-ins

There are many ways of displaying data on the Web, such as 3-D animation or video clips, and they need special small programs to run them. Rather than having to develop a whole new browser to cope with these file formats, software developers will write these plug-ins to integrate into your browser. When a browser locates one of these files it will run the plug-in to enable the file to be displayed or viewed within your browser. Some plug-ins are already integrated into the browser, such as Shockwave for animated graphics, and are installed along with the browser. Others can be downloaded from web sites and installed on your computer much like you might install any other program. Adobe® Acrobat Reader® is an example of a plug-in which can be freely downloaded and used to read documents produced in a format called portable document format (pdf). It isn't usually necessary to install a plug-in until you run into a web page that requires it and you will often find that these web pages include instructions for downloading and installing the plug-in you need.

Some of the plug-ins you may find useful are:

Players

 Flash Player
View rich content and applications with the leading rich client.

 Shockwave Player
View entertaining rich-media and 3D web content.

Shockwave and **Flash** are used to play multimedia presentations, games, and animations (http://www.macromedia.com/).

 RealPlayer is used to play music and voice files (RealAudio) and video files (RealVideo). Streaming technology is used for these players so you don't have to download the whole file before starting to play it (http://www.real.com/).

 **WinAmp** is used to play MP3 music files. MP3 files are CD quality and take up relatively little room on your hard drive (http://www.winamp.com).

QuickTime can be used to play video clips in Apple's QuickTime format (http://www.apple.com/).

IPIX viewer is produced by Interactive Pictures Corporation and enables you to view 360° panoramic images as if you were standing in the middle of the scene (http://www.ipix.com/). Apple's QuickTimeVR is another format used for panoramic images (http://apple.com/quicktime/qtvr/).

Acrobat Reader® is used to view documents produced in Adobe's pdf format (http://www.adobe.com/).

E-mail software

E-mail software allows you to compose and send messages and receive messages in return. There are several e-mail programs, but the most popular are **Outlook Express** and **Netscape Messenger**. This software is often included on the CD-ROMs provided by ISPs, although you can download both of them from either the Microsoft web site or the Netscape web site. Outlook Express is also included in the Windows Operating System and may already be loaded onto your computer. Two of the other popular e-mail programs are Eudora and Pegasus, and although these may all look slightly different in appearance when in use, they will all perform many of the same functions.

As with browser software, new versions of e-mail programs are being developed and released all the time. It is always worth checking the web sites now and again to download the latest version which will usually have more features and functions.

Connection software

To connect to the Internet you will need some software to allow your modem to connect your computer to the global network that is the Internet. This software is called **Dial-Up Networking (DUN)** and setting up this program is often part of the process in the software provided by your ISP. This small program stores your ISP details and controls your modem. Your ISP's set-up disc will check to see if DUN is installed on your machine already. If it finds that it isn't installed it will ask you to insert your Windows CD.

If you need to install it yourself, you will need your Windows CD at the ready.

Method

1   From the **Start** button select the **Settings** option.
2   Select **Control Panel** from the menu.
3   Double click on the **Add/Remove Programs** icon.
4   Click the **Windows Setup** tab in the dialogue box.
5   Select **Dial-Up Networking** from the **Components** list (located under **Communications**).
6   Select it and click **OK** twice.
7   Follow the onscreen instructions which will prompt you to insert your Windows CD to install Dial-Up Networking.

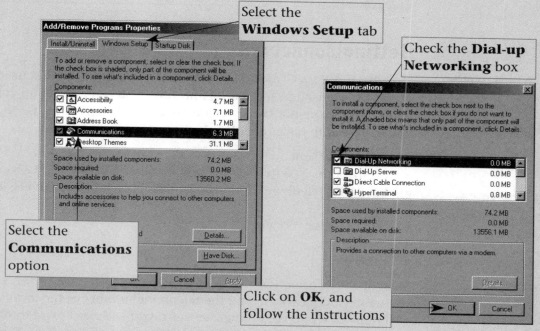

Figure 1.9 Installing dial-up networking

Note: You may have to re-start your computer for the changes to take effect after you have finished the installation.

→ Check your knowledge 1

1   What equipment do you need to connect to the Internet?
2   Answer the following True or False:

   a A computer needs to have at least a 1 GHz processor to connect to the Internet.

   b Broadband can transfer data at speeds of 512 Kbps or more.

   c ISDN and Home Highway are only available if you live in a big city.

   d A leased line is a cheap option for a home user.

   e ADSL stands for Asymmetric Digital Subscriber Line.

3 With a broadband connection, how many minutes (approximately) would it take to download a 6.4 MB file?

4 What type of modem would you use to connect to an ADSL line?

5 What type of file is 'streamed'? Why is a broadband connection better for this type of file?

6 How could you check your connection speed?

7 What might you need to consider when choosing an ISP?

8 Why would you use a browser when connecting to the Internet?

9 What are 'plug-ins'?

10 What is the difference between a browser and an e-mail program?

Getting connected

Usually your ISP's CD will be configured with all the settings needed to make the connection to your ISP, however you can also set up your connection using the **Internet Connection Wizard**. To use this method you will need to have the following information to hand:

- Your ISP's name
- Connection type (phone line and modem, ISDN, ADSL, LAN)
- Your ISP's telephone number (the one to access their servers, not their Helpline!)
- Details of the modem
- Username
- Password.

Most of the information you need will be provided by your ISP, such as your username and password, and the telephone number of the local host. If you also want to set up your e-mail account, you will need extra information which will also be provided by your ISP:

- Your e-mail address
- The addresses of your ISP's mail servers

Task 1.2	Setting up your connection using your ISP's CD-ROM method

Method

I Switch on the computer and load the operating system.

2 Put the CD in the CD drive. Most computers are set up to automatically run (autorun) the CD when the drive tray is closed. If nothing happens, you may need to start it yourself.
  a Double click on **My Computer**.
  b Double click on the icon for your CD-ROM drive.
  c Double click on the icon that says **Setup**.

3 Select the **Install** option from any menus that appear in the open window. The screen may look similar to the one below

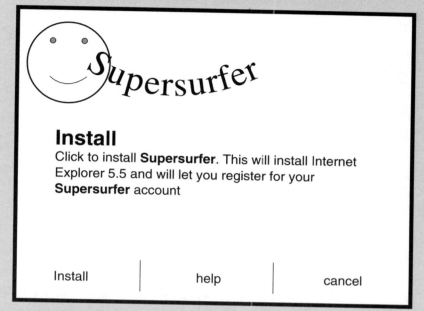

Figure 1.10 Installing software

4 If a licence agreement box appears, click on the button next to the **I accept the agreement** (you should read this first though). Click on **Next**.

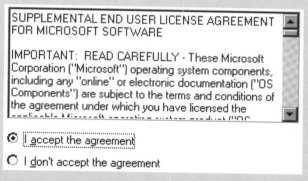

Figure 1.11 A licence agreement

5 When the software has been installed, which may take a few minutes, you will be informed that the program is going to **reset** (close down and restart) your computer. Click on the appropriate option to accept (this could be something like **Finish** or **OK**).

6 After your computer has reset, you will find the welcome screen of your ISP which will guide you through the setup process for your account. Follow the instructions on screen, which may look something like the following screens:

Note:

You may need to choose your modem from a dialogue box.

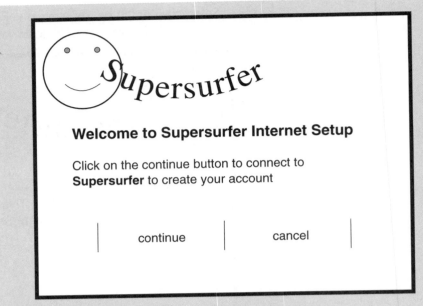

Welcome to Supersurfer Internet Setup

Click on the continue button to connect to
Supersurfer to create your account

| continue | cancel |

Figure 1.12 The sort of screen that welcomes you to an ISP

7   At some point you will need to enter some personal details and make
     your choice of e-mail address and password. The screen may look
     similar to the one shown, but will be individual for each provider.

Supersurfer

Personal Information

First Name

Last Name

Male ☐   Female ☐

Date of Birth   /   /

House name
or number

Street

Town/City

County/Postcode

| continue | cancel |

Figure 1.13 A screen like this shows the sort of information needed to set up an e-mail
address and password

8 Your computer may dial up your new ISP to complete the registration procedure. Don't worry about the strange screeching noises your modem might make – it's just part of the connection process.

Information

When you choose your e-mail address, you may find that you will have to make a second choice if someone else has already chosen the one you want. It's a good idea to have a few other suggestions ready, just in case.

9 Once all the signing up is done, you can access your browser by double clicking on the appropriate icon on your desktop. This may be the Internet Explorer icon or the Netscape Navigator icon, or maybe an icon which your ISP provides through their software.

Information

Don't forget to make a note of your e-mail address and your password. You might be reminded by the software, but make sure that you keep your password safe from other eyes.

Task 1.3   Setting up your connection manually

Method

I   Using the **Start** menu, locate and select the **Internet Connection Wizard**.

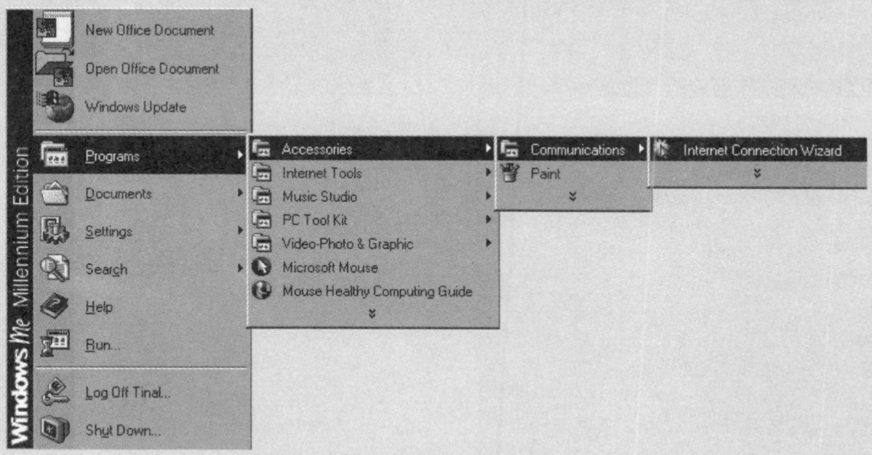

Figure 1.14 Selecting Internet Connection Wizard

Note: Click on **Next** after completing each screen.

2 Select the appropriate option from the **Welcome** dialogue box

Figure 1.15 Welcome dialogue box

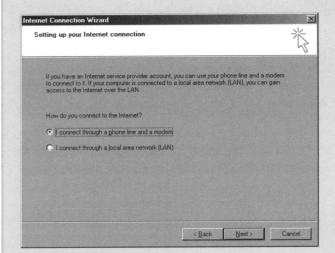

Figure 1.16 Setting up your Internet connection

3 Select how you want to connect to the Internet. If you're connecting from home, it will probably be the '**connect through a phone line and a modem**' option.

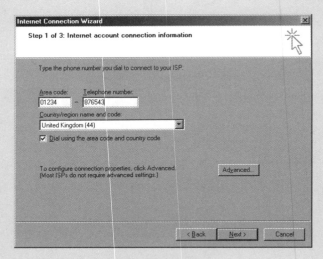

Figure 1.17 Enter phone number

4 Enter the phone number of your ISP and check that the country is correct.

5 Enter your username and your password.

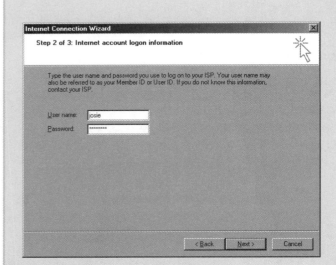

Figure 1.18 Enter logon information

6 Give your connection a name.

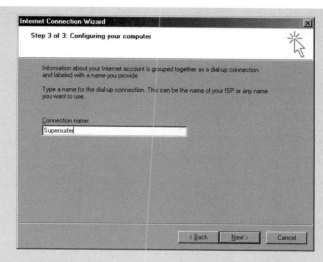

Figure 1.19 Connection name

7 Select the appropriate option – **Yes** if you want to set up your e-mail account.

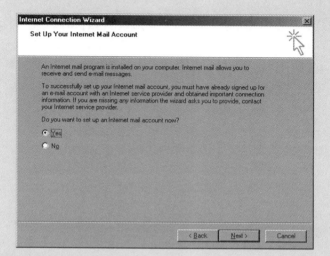

Figure 1.20 Setting up e-mail account

8 Select the appropriate option – this will depend on whether you're setting up a new account or using an existing one.

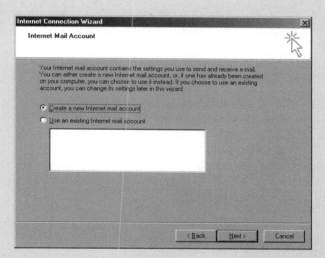

Figure 1.21 Selecting e-mail option

9 Enter the name and you want for your account.

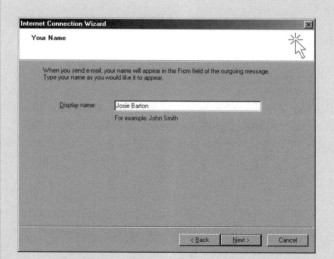

Figure 1.22 Entering your e-mail account name

10 Enter your e-mail address – this may be given to you by your ISP.

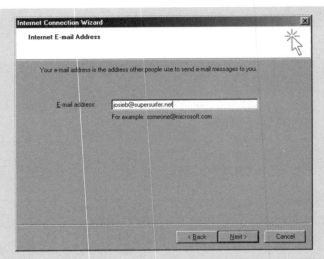

Figure 1.23 Entering your e-mail address

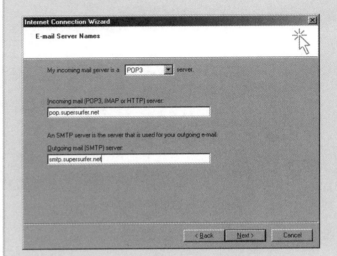

Figure 1.24 Entering e-mail server details

11 Enter your mail server details – these should be given to you by your ISP.

12 Enter your account name and your password provided by your ISP.

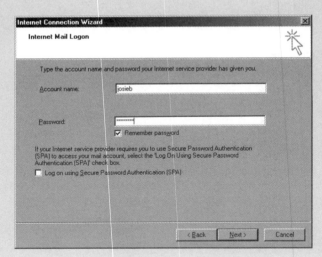

Figure 1.25 Entering account name and password

Figure 1.26 Connecting to your ISP

13 Connect to your ISP and you'll soon be able to start sending your e-mails!

You are now ready to connect to your ISP and begin to explore the mine of information available on the Internet. To enhance your surfing experience you may decide that you want to change the way your web pages are viewed and to set up your browser to suit your own preferences. Most browsers will allow you to change some of the settings to enable you to customise your browser window.

Viewing web pages

Changing the appearance of web pages

Screen resolution

Your screen image is made up of little squares called pixels (picture elements). The more squares there are, the clearer the image will be. Resolution values are shown in pixels and the resolution on your screen can be changed using the **Display Properties** box.

Task 1.4   Changing the screen resolution

Method

1   Right click the mouse on a blank area of the screen.
2   Select **Properties** from the pop-up menu.
3   Select the **Settings** tab from the **Display Properties** dialogue box.
4   Move the slider for the **Screen area** until the best view for you is shown in the preview box.
5   Click on **Apply**.
6   The screen will flicker and the new settings will be displayed.
7   Click **OK** to accept the changes.

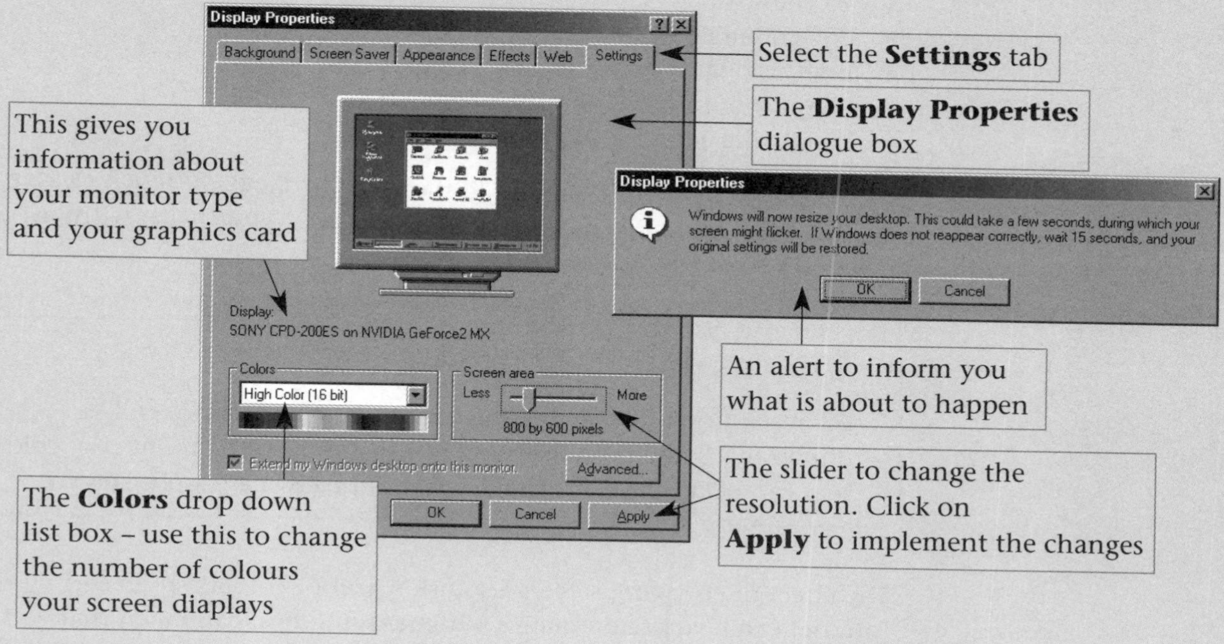

This gives you information about your monitor type and your graphics card

Select the **Settings** tab

The **Display Properties** dialogue box

Windows will now resize your desktop. This could take a few seconds, during which your screen might flicker. If Windows does not reappear correctly, wait 15 seconds, and your original settings will be restored.

An alert to inform you what is about to happen

The slider to change the resolution. Click on **Apply** to implement the changes

The **Colors** drop down list box – use this to change the number of colours your screen diaplays

Figure 1.27 Changing screen resolution

Resolutions and colours

The lowest screen area value is 640 × 480 pixels. This means that your image is made up of a grid of 640 columns and 480 rows. That is quite a total of pixels on your screen – over 300,000! However, if your monitor and video adapter (sometimes called video card, graphics card or display adapter) can support a greater resolution (more pixels), you could select up to 1600 × 1200.

- The more pixels you use, the smaller things will look on the screen. On the other hand, you will be able to see more on your screen so you've effectively enlarged your viewing area.
- The greater the resolution, the higher the demand for computer resources. This could slow down your computer.
- Some generally accepted settings for different sizes of screen are:

Screen size	Maximum resolution
14″	640 × 480
15″	800 × 600
17″	1024 × 768
19–21″	1280 × 1024 or 1600 × 1200

The Settings tab also gives access to the number of colours you can have displayed. The **Colors** (note the American spelling without the 'u') drop down list box will allow you to select various colour options. The options may be:

- 16 colours
- 256 colours
- high colour (16-bit or 65,536 colours)
- 24-bit true colour (16 million colours)
- 32-bit true colour (even more colours!)

Obviously a picture, especially a photograph, will appear much clearer and be a higher quality image with 16-bit or higher colours than with just 16 colours.

The effect of changing screen resolution and/or colours when surfing the Internet can be quite dramatic. A higher resolution can mean that you can get more of the web page on your desktop, which means less scrolling to see bits that are off the screen. It will mean that the text and images are smaller and you may need to try different settings to get a resolution which you find easy to view. A lower resolution will give you larger text and images, but they may be more 'blocky' and less smooth in appearance. The number of colours displayed will affect the quality of the images you see.

Another factor with higher resolution and large numbers of colours is the amount of computing power that is used. Higher resolution and/or a greater number of colours means the processor will have to work harder and consequently may mean your computer works more slowly. Getting the right balance between resolution, colour and power use is a fine balance, unless your computer has masses of processing power and RAM, of course!

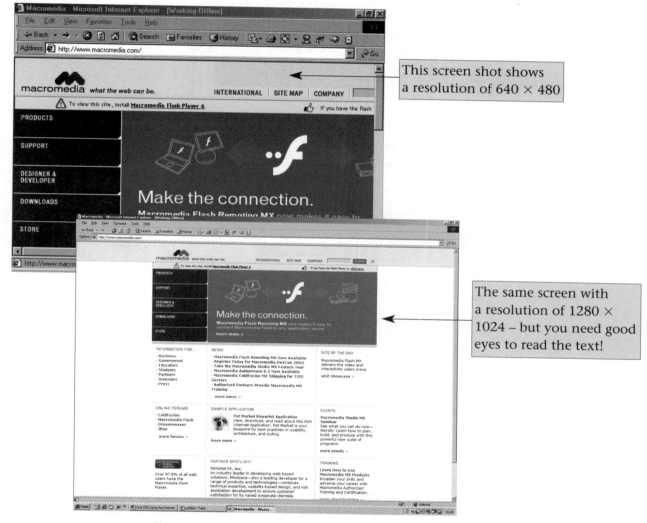

This screen shot shows a resolution of 640 × 480

The same screen with a resolution of 1280 × 1024 – but you need good eyes to read the text!

Figure 1.28 Screen resolutions

Loading web pages faster

There are other options in Explorer that can be used to change the appearance of web pages which may help to load them faster. For example, turning off the options for downloading images, sounds, etc. can make the pages load noticeably quicker.

Task 1.5 | Turning off graphics, videos, sounds, animations in web pages

Method

1   Select the **Internet Options** from the **Tools** menu.
2   Select the **Advanced** tab.
3   Scroll down to the **Multimedia** heading and uncheck the required boxes for **Show pictures, Play animations**, **Play videos**, or **Play sounds**.
4   Click on **Apply** to make the changes, or **Cancel** if you change your mind!

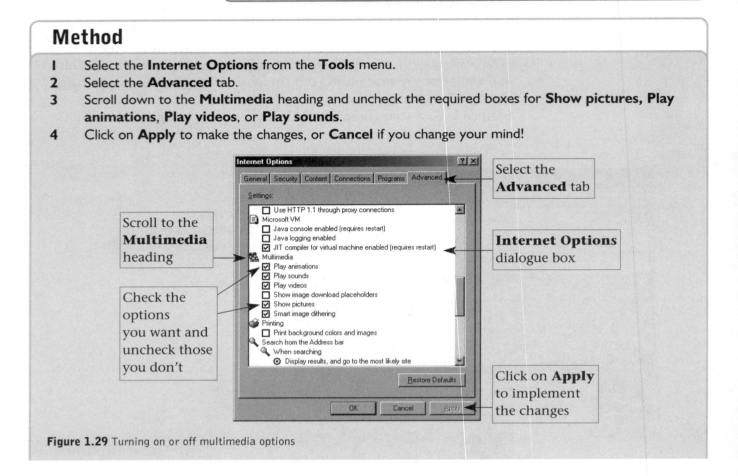

Scroll to the **Multimedia** heading

Check the options you want and uncheck those you don't

Select the **Advanced** tab

Internet Options dialogue box

Click on **Apply** to implement the changes

Figure 1.29 Turning on or off multimedia options

Information

You can turn any of the multimedia options on again by checking the appropriate boxes.

Information

If the **Show pictures** or **Display videos** option is unchecked, you can still display an individual picture or animation on a web page by right clicking its icon and then selecting **Show Picture** from the pop-up menu.

If you find the pictures are still visible after unchecking the **Show pictures** box, select **Refresh** from the **View** menu to hide them.

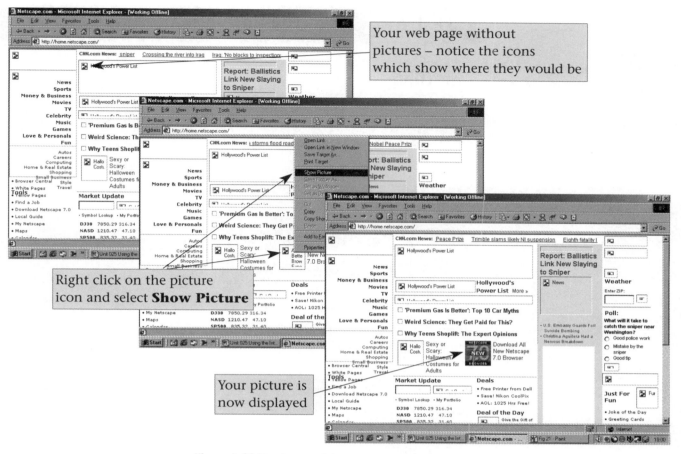

Your web page without pictures – notice the icons which show where they would be

Right click on the picture icon and select **Show Picture**

Your picture is now displayed

Figure 1.30 Turning on pictures

Getting the full picture!

When you load your browser and connect to the Net, you may find that your toolbars (more about them later) get in the way of what you want to view. Using the **F11** key will give you a full screen view with just your Standard toolbar shown at the top of the screen. To restore your original view complete with all toolbars, simply press the F11 key again. You can also access the **Full Screen** option from the **View** menu.

Customising your browser

Toolbars and menus

You can change the appearance and location of the Menu bar, Standard buttons, Address bar and Links bar. You can move buttons around, add buttons or remove buttons, move toolbars and make the icons bigger or smaller – in fact there are several options for customising your toolbars to suit you.

Menu bar

Address bar

Standard toolbar

Links bar

Figure 1.31 Options for customising toolbars

Method

1   Right click on an empty section of the toolbar.
2   Select or deselect the appropriate toolbar from the pop-up menu which appears.

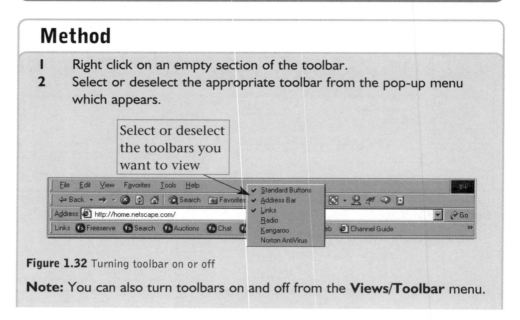

Figure 1.32 Turning toolbar on or off

Note: You can also turn toolbars on and off from the **Views/Toolbar** menu.

Method

1   Click and hold the mouse button on the grey handle at left-hand side of the toolbar (your cursor will change to an arrow-headed cross).
2   Drag the toolbar to where you want to place it and release the mouse button. You can move the toolbar up, down, right or left.

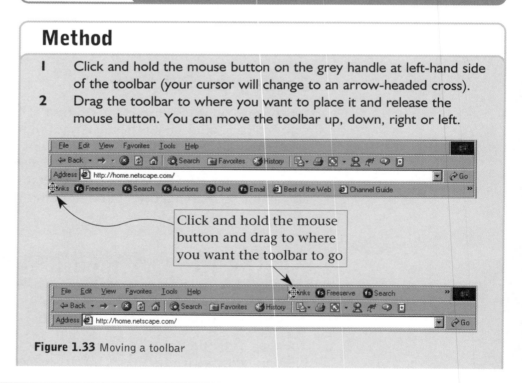

Figure 1.33 Moving a toolbar

Information

The toolbars have to be at the top of the window – you can't turn them into floating tool palettes, or move them to the side or the bottom of the window.

You can have more than one toolbar on the same line. If there is no room to show all the buttons on the toolbar, a double arrow button will be shown. Clicking on this button will give access to the other buttons.

Note:

You can unlock the toolbars using the same method but deselect the **Lock the Toolbar** option.

This option is only available in Internet Explorer Version 6.

Task 1.8 Locking the toolbars (Internet Explorer Version 6)

Method

I   Right click on an empty section of the toolbar.
2   Select **Lock the Toolbar** option from the drop down menu which appears.

Task 1.9 Customising the Standard toolbar

Method

I   Right click in a blank space on the **Standard toolbar**.
2   Select **Customize** (American spelling!) from the pop-up menu.

The **Customize Toolbar** dialogue box will enable you to make changes to the way your toolbar looks.

- The **Available toolbar buttons** pane shows the buttons which are available to add to the toolbar, the **Current toolbar buttons** pane shows the button currently on the toolbar.
- In the **Available toolbar buttons** pane dialogue box select the toolbar button you wish to add to the toolbar and click the **Add** button. The selected button will move to the Current toolbar buttons pane. To remove a button, select it in the Current toolbar buttons pane and click on **Remove**.
- You can choose large or small icons for your toolbar from the **Icon options** drop down list box.
- By selecting options from the **Text options** drop down list box you can change the labels on your toolbar buttons. You can even have no text shown, which will make your toolbar look very like those in Word.
- You can change the order of buttons on the toolbar by selecting a button and clicking **Move Up** or **Move Down**.

3   Click on **Close** to finish, or **Reset** to undo any changes you may have made.

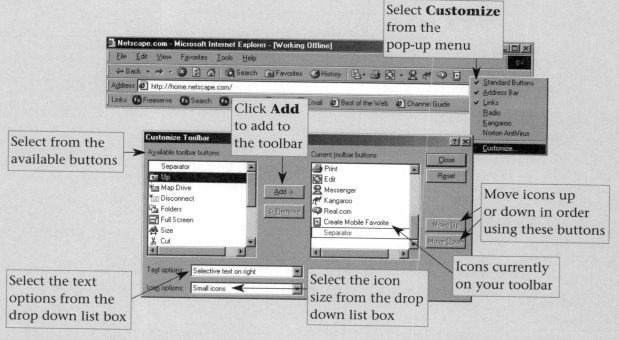

Figure 1.34 Customising the toolbar

Task 1.10 Adding links to the Links bar

Note:

To rearrange items on the Links bar, click and hold the mouse button on the link and drag to a new location on the bar.

Method

1 Click and hold down the mouse button on a web page link.
2 Drag the link to the **Links** toolbar.
3 Release the mouse button.

Your homepage

Homepage can have two meanings. It can be the front page of a web site or it can be the page you have as your opening screen when you load your browser. More often than not, your opening page when you load your browser will be the front page of your ISP. You don't have to keep that as your homepage, however, and changing it is very straightforward.

Task 1.11 Changing your homepage

Method

1 Click on **Start**.
2 Navigate the menu and select **Settings/Control Panel**.
3 Double click on the **Internet Options**.
4 Select the **General** tab.
5 Enter the URL of the web page you want as your homepage.
6 Click on **Apply** and **OK**.

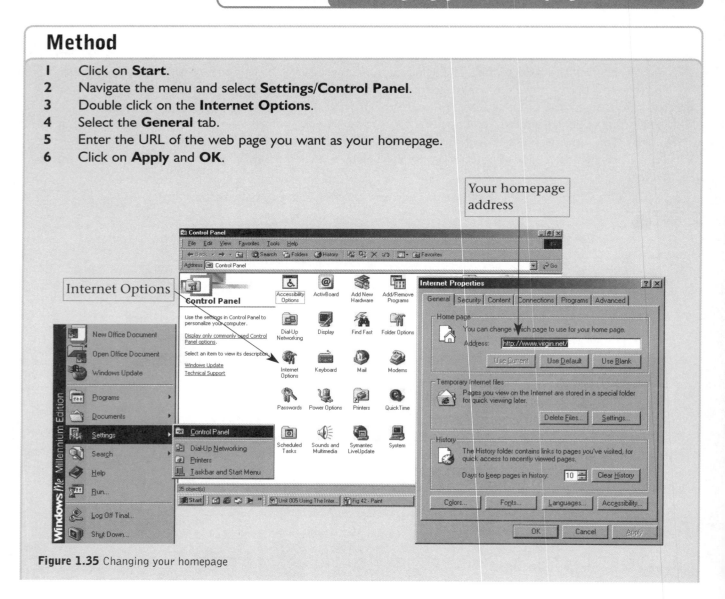

Figure 1.35 Changing your homepage

Setting security

Your browser and e-mail programs have security features which will also help in the fight against viruses. In the Internet Options dialogue box you can specify how Internet Explorer should handle the downloading of files, depending on where they have come from.

Task 1.12 — Setting your security levels

Method

1 Select **Internet Options** from the **Tools** menu.
2 Select the **Security** tab.

You will see that four security zones are shown:

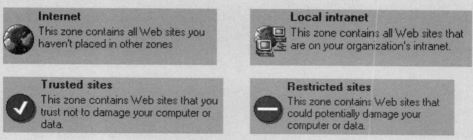

Internet
This zone contains all Web sites you haven't placed in other zones

Local intranet
This zone contains all Web sites that are on your organization's intranet.

Trusted sites
This zone contains Web sites that you trust not to damage your computer or data.

Restricted sites
This zone contains Web sites that could potentially damage your computer or data.

Figure 1.36 Security zones

You can assign different levels of security to each zone.

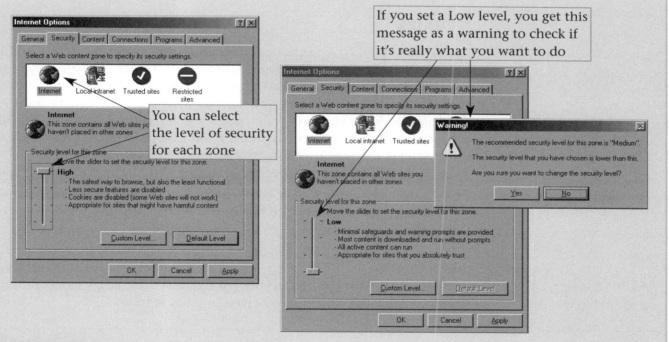

You can select the level of security for each zone

If you set a Low level, you get this message as a warning to check if it's really what you want to do

Figure 1.37 Setting security levels

The higher the level of security, the less likely you are to be able to download files containing a virus. You can add sites to all of the zones except the Internet one, which contains all the sites not listed in any other category.

3 Select the levels of security which you feel are appropriate for your needs.

Information

Outlook Express shares the settings with Internet Explorer and has a similar function as shown in the screen shot in Figure 1.39.

Select the zone you require by checking the box

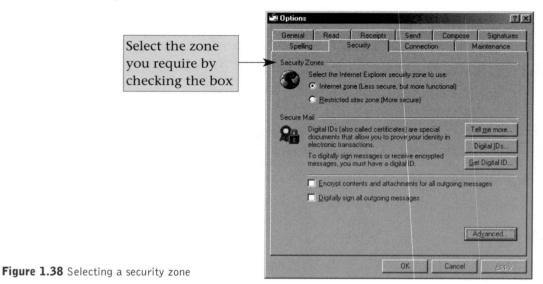

Figure 1.38 Selecting a security zone

Cookies

In computer terms cookies can be both a benefit and a nuisance. You may visit web sites that store information as a small text file on your computer. These are called **cookies**. Internet sites use them to store personal information about such things as your preferences when visiting their site. This might be the particular pages you visited or your name if you entered it into any boxes whilst at the site. When you next log on to the site your computer sends the cookie to the site and you may find a message appearing which says 'Hello, Josie. Welcome back.' Cookies can't be used to read data from your hard drive, to pass on your personal details or to make sure the software on your machine has been registered. They are not really harmful, although whether you want them cluttering up your hard drive is a matter for you to decide.

One way of making sure that all cookies don't settle themselves on your hard drive is to set the levels of security in your zones to suit you. For example, you might want to allow web sites in your Trusted zone to create cookies or prompt you to ask for permission if they are in your Internet zone.

Information

You can change your computer settings to disable cookies being stored on your computer using the **Internet Options**. By selecting **Custom Level** from the dialogue box, you can change the cookie settings by checking the appropriate box as shown in the screen shot below: →

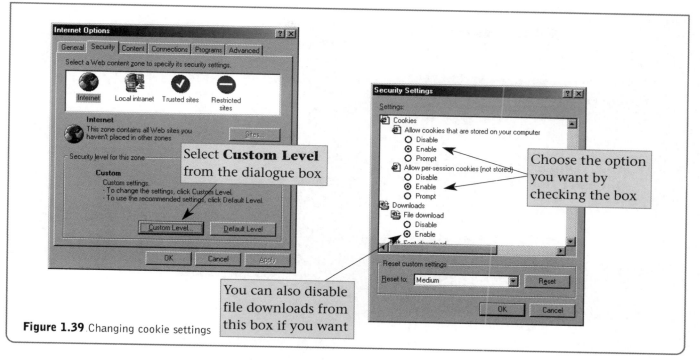

Figure 1.39 Changing cookie settings

Cache settings

Many browsers will store web pages on your hard drive in an area called the **cache**. If you have previously visited a web page and a copy is placed in your cache, when you return to the page your browser will check on your hard drive to see if the page is in your cache and load it from there. This can make surfing much easier and quicker as the browser doesn't have to check with the ISP's server to get a copy of the page.

All these pages stored on your hard drive can take up quite a lot of space and you can set the size of your cache to suit your requirements. If you only have a small hard drive, this may be a useful option to save some space. Internet Explorer will store these copies of web pages in the **Temporary Internet files** folder.

Task 1.13 **Changing your cache settings**

Method

1 Select **Internet Options** from the **Tools** menu.
2 Select the **General** tab.
3 Click on **Settings** from the **Temporary Internet files** section.
- You can select how Explorer checks for newer versions of web pages. You may want it to check on every visit to the page, in which case that is the option to select.
- The amount of disk space used by Temporary Internet files can be adjusted by moving the slider under the **Amount of disk space to use** heading. The amount of space devoted to storing these files can be seen in the box alongside the slider.
- The **Move Folder** button will allow you to change the folder where these temporary files are stored.
- Clicking the **View Files** button will allow you to see a list of the web and graphic files stored in the folder.
- If you want to see the other web-related files such as ActiveX controls, the **View Objects** button will allow you to access them.

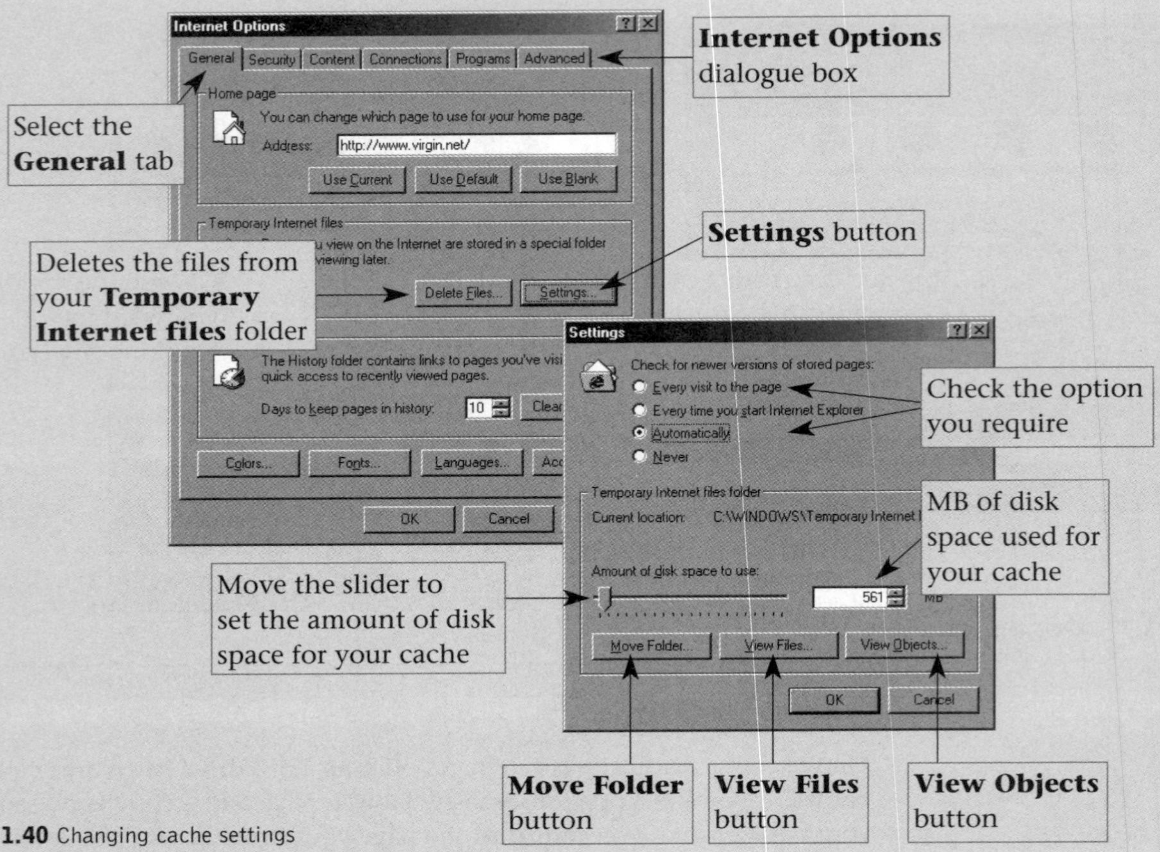
Internet Options
dialogue box
Select the
General tab
Settings button
Deletes the files from
your Temporary
Internet files folder
Check the option
you require
MB of disk
space used for
your cache
Move the slider to
set the amount of disk
space for your cache
Move Folder
button
View Files
button
View Objects
button

Figure 1.40 Changing cache settings

> **Note:**
>
> When you open your **History** folder in Internet Explorer, you will notice that some of the icons appear solid whilst others are ghostly images of the icons. If the page is cached, the icon will appear solid and can be loaded whilst you are offline. You cannot load a page from History if the icon appears as a pale image.

> **Note:**
>
> Evaluation versions of WinZip can be obtained from www.winzip.com. PKZip can be obtained from www.pkware.com.

You may have noticed the **Delete Files** button next to **Settings** in the Temporary Internet files section of the Internet Properties box. Clicking this button will delete all the files in your Temporary Internet files folder.

Compression/decompression software

If you are sending files over the Internet, especially large graphic files, they can take quite some time to upload, as will large image files you may want to download from the Web. Using compression/decompression software (called **archive programs**) can be very useful to squeeze large files into much smaller files. This will obviously make uploading or downloading quicker and could make it less likely that you will lose files. Software available for download on the Net is often in a compressed format – saving time and money. Compressing files is frequently referred to as 'zipping' a file. Two of the most popular programs for doing this are **WinZip** and **PKZip**. These programs are often found on computer magazine cover discs, or they can be downloaded from the Net. They are shareware programs, which means you can try them out for a short time before deciding whether you want to keep them. If you want to carry on using them you would pay the software company for a full licence.

Archive programs can also be used to compress files on your hard drive to save space. This can be a handy option if you find that your hard drive is rapidly filling up!

Method

1   Log on to your ISP and enter the URL for the WinZip web site in the Address bar.
2   Click on the download link for the evaluation copy.
3   Select the **Save this program to disk** option from the **File Download** dialogue box.
4   Browse your hard drive to find an appropriate place to save the file and click **OK** (don't change the file name offered).
5   Disconnect from the Internet when the **Download complete** dialogue box appears.

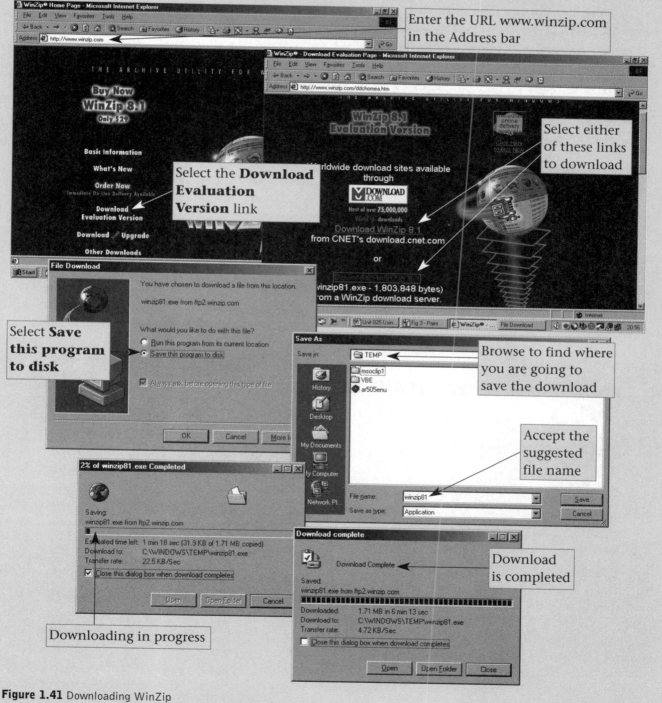

Figure 1.41 Downloading WinZip

Method

1. Locate the saved file on your hard drive.
2. Double click on the file – it will be called something like winzip81.exe.
3. Click on the **Setup** button in the dialogue box which appears.
4. Follow the onscreen instructions to install your software (it's probably best to accept the suggestion for the folder unless you need to change it).
5. Click on the **Next** buttons in the following dialogue boxes until the **Select 'Wizard' or 'Classic'** option box appears (and make sure you read and accept the licence agreement!).

   The 'Wizard' interface does some of the basic tasks for you, but the 'Classic' interface is quite easy to use. If you select 'Classic', you can always change to 'Wizard' at a later date.

6. Click on **Next** to continue.
7. Select **Express setup** from the following dialogue box and click on **Next**.
8. Click on **Next** to associate your archive files with WinZip (this means that all archive files will open in WinZip unless you change the file association).
9. Click on **Finish** and WinZip should be ready to use.

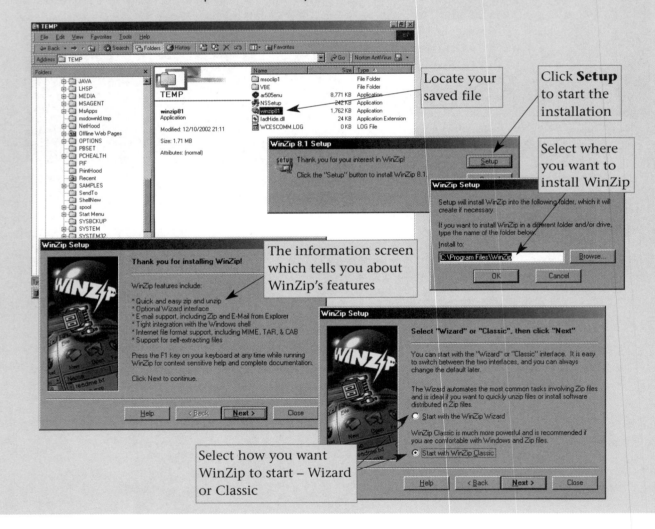

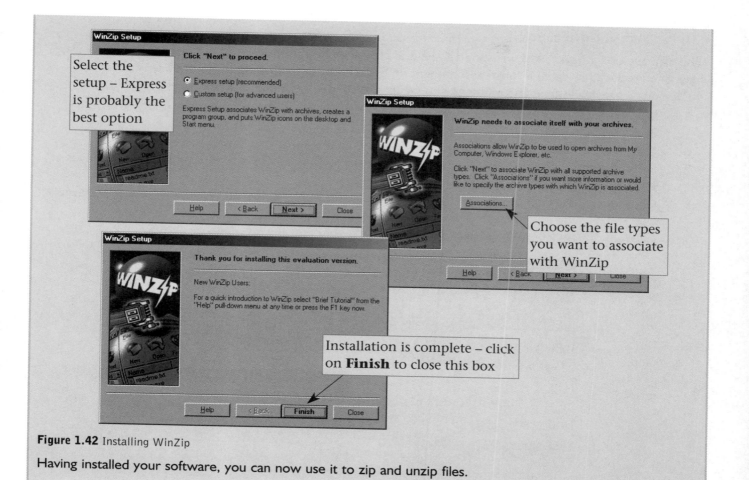

Figure 1.42 Installing WinZip

Having installed your software, you can now use it to zip and unzip files.

Information

You can recognise a WinZip file by the icon.

Many of the zipped files you may download from the Web will be 'self-extracting' – that means they carry their own program to install the files. Most archive files will have an extension such as .zip, .cab, .tar, .gzip.

Task 1.16 — Opening an archive with WinZip

Note: The following method and screen shots use WinZip, although many of the steps are similar in other compression/decompression programs.

Method

1. Load WinZip (either double click the WinZip icon on your desktop or use the Start/Programs/WinZip menu options).
2. Click the **Open** button on the toolbar (or select **Open Archive** from the **File** menu).
3. In the **Open Archive** dialogue box, browse your hard drive to find the file you wish to unzip and select it.

4   Click the **Open** button.

The dialogue box which opens will show all the files contained in the zip file. You will notice that all the files have been reduced by quite a substantial amount. In the screen shot shown, one file has been reduced by 40% – quite a saving in time and money if you wanted to send it as an e-mail attachment!

5   Select the file you want to extract (select more by holding down the **Control** key and clicking on each file you want).

6   Click the **Extract** button on the toolbar (or select **Extract** from the **Actions** menu).

7   In the **Extract** dialogue box, select where you want to save the file by browsing the Folders/drives in the pane to the right.

8   Choose any other options you want – the example shown has **Selected files** and **Use folder names** checked.

9   Click the **Extract** button and your files will be extracted into the location you chose.

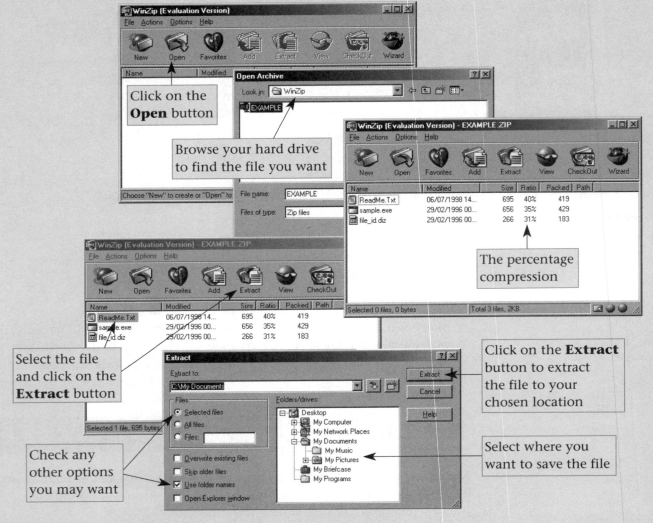

Figure 1.43 Opening an archive with WinZip

Method

1   When you have reached step 4 above, you may wish to view what's in the files to make sure they contain the information you want. In the dialogue box select the file you wish to view.
2   Click the **View** button on the toolbar.
3   Select the option you would like to use to view the file. (It's usually best to view the file in its associated program although you may have to choose the **Viewer** option if it doesn't have one and make your own suggestion.)

Information

All files are **associated** with a program, which is often the program in which they were produced. When you double click on the file in Windows Explorer or from My Computer, it will open in the program with which it is associated. Some programs will open many different file types and files can be associated with programs other than the one in which they were created. You can tell which program created the file by the extension, which is shown by the last three letters after the file name. For example, minutes.doc would have been produced in Word, which adds the .doc extension when you save your file.

4   Click on the **View** button.

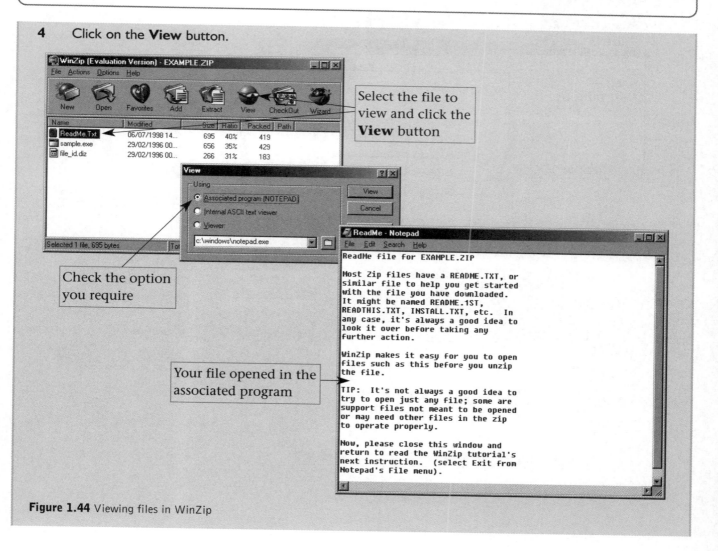

Figure 1.44 Viewing files in WinZip

Method

1   Load the WinZip program.
2   Click on the **New** button (or select **New Archive** from the **File** menu).
3   In the **New Archive** dialogue box select the folder where you want to create your zip file.
4   Name your zip file in the **File name** box (this is the name of the archive, not the files you will be compressing).
5   Make sure the **Add dialog** option at the bottom of the dialogue box is checked.
6   Click on **OK**.
7   In the **Add** dialogue box which appears, browse your folders to find the files you want to add to the archive.
8   Select the file (or files by using the **Ctrl** key and clicking on each file you want to add) and click the **Add** button. Your files will be listed in the WinZip window and you can check to see how much the files have been compressed.
9   Add any other files to the archive using the same steps as above.
10   Close the WinZip program when you have finished.

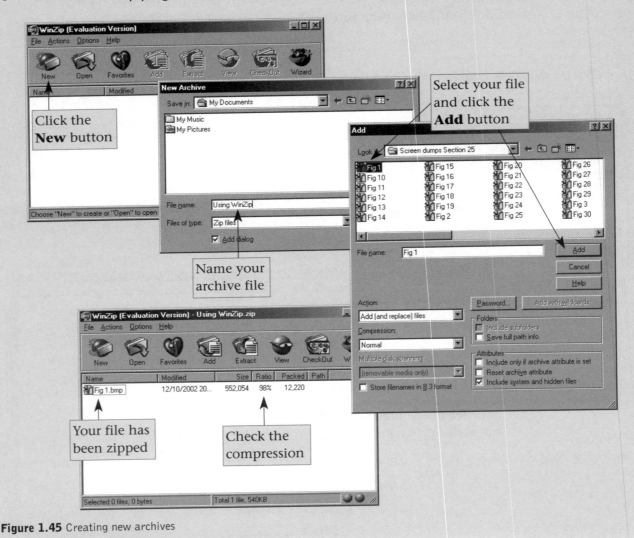

Figure 1.45 Creating new archives

Information

Sending one zip file containing many different files, which could include text documents, images, video clips, etc., as an e-mail attachment would be much neater than sending each file individually, as well as saving time and money.

→ Practise your skills 1

1 Connect to the Internet and search for three different ISPs.
2 Compare the information from the ISP checklist to decide which is the best option for your needs.
3 Reload the web page of the ISP you have chosen and turn off the graphics. Take a screen capture of the web page and print out a copy.
4 Add a link to this page to your Links bar and take a screen capture. Print out a copy.
5 Use the full page view and then restore to normal view.
6 Set your homepage as www.bbc.co.uk. Take a screen capture of the settings dialogue box to show this and print out a copy.
7 Close your browser and disconnect from the Internet.

→ Practise your skills 2

1 Check your cache settings and note down the details.
2 Set the security for Internet Explorer to high and take a screen capture. Print out a copy.
3 Disable cookies from being downloaded.
4 Clear the History and Temporary Internet files. Take a screen capture of the settings box and print out a copy.

→ Practise your skills 3

1 Change your screen resolution to the lowest setting.
2 Connect to your ISP and take a screen capture. Print out a copy.
3 Turn off the Address bar and rearrange the Standard toolbar so it is at the bottom of the toolbar array.
4 Minimise your browser window and alter the screen resolution to the highest setting available.
5 Restore your browser window and take a screen capture. Print out a copy.
6 Close your browser and disconnect from the Internet.
7 Restore your display settings to your own preference.

→ Practise your skills 4

1 Connect to the Internet.

2 Download and install WinZip (if it isn't already installed on your machine).

3 Close your browser and disconnect from the Internet.

4 Either select three Word files and one bitmap file saved on your hard drive, or create them (if you have to create them, they only need to be very simple documents).

5 Create and save an archive with the name **test archive** using WinZip which contains the four files.

6 View the files and note down the percentage compression for each file.

7 Close WinZip.

8 Open WinZip and locate your archive file.

9 Unzip the files to a new location on your hard drive.

10 Close WinZip.

→ Check your knowledge 2

1 What information will you need to set up your connection to your ISP manually?

2 Why might you need to alter your screen resolution?

3 What effect will turning off graphics, etc. have on the way web pages are loaded?

4 How would you turn off a toolbar?

5 What steps would you need to take to add a link to the Links bar?

6 How many security zones are there in Internet Explorer, and what are they?

7 What advantages might there be in setting the level of security in Internet Explorer to high?

8 Cookies are beneficial. Discuss this.

9 What are the benefits of changing the cache settings?

10 Why might you use compression/decompression software?

Section 2 | Accessing all areas

You will learn to

- Describe the services available via the Internet
  - ☐ WWW
  - ☐ e-mail
  - ☐ newsgroups
  - ☐ talk and chat
  - ☐ FTP
  - ☐ Telnet
  - ☐ e-commerce
  - ☐ audio/video conferencing
  - ☐ data conferencing
  - ☐ desktop sharing
- Access WWW using search engines with simple and complex criteria
- Navigate web pages
- Locate and download shareware and freeware programs, saving to a specified location
- Use FTP software to transfer files
- Participate in relevant newsgroups
- Participate in a chat session
- Describe the relevance and implications of the Internet

The Internet

The Internet is the world's largest network with many millions of computers joined together by cables, satellites and phone lines. Joining this network, with a PC and the minimum of equipment, is a fairly straightforward process which won't cost you a great deal of money. Once you have connected to this super network you can access and share information in many different ways. Electronic mail (e-mail), documents, articles, books, images, film and music are amongst some of the most popular ways of exchanging data, but new ways of sending information are being developed all the time.

Some of the Internet services you can access are:

WWW – The World Wide Web

The Web, as the **World Wide Web** is usually called, is made up of over a billion pages written in HTML (HyperText Markup Language) and developed by people all over the world. The number of pages is growing all the time and they could come from academic institutions, governments, companies and businesses, local and national (and even international) organisations, in fact the list is endless – they could even be from you! Web pages contain mostly text, images, graphics, photos, video and sound clips, with documents from all parts of the world linked to one another to form part of a giant 'hypertext' system. Clicking on a hyperlink in a web page can take you halfway across the world in seconds. The millions of pages on the Web are presented in a variety of ways and may contain:

- **Video and animation**   Links on a web page may take you to a video clip, which could be from a recent film release, perhaps, or from a music video. Sometimes animation sequences are added to web pages to make them more interesting.
- **Information**   You can find out about almost anything on the Web, from the information you need to complete a project to what your stars have in store for you today. One of the best known uses for the Web is research, but it doesn't stop there, because the Web can be updated so quickly you can find out the latest news, a weather forecast for your area, your team's latest score and the price of your shares, all at the touch of button. You can search for your ideal job and check out the company before your interview from the comfort of your own home.
- **Software**   Links are often provided to enable you to download programs which you can install on your computer. These could be plug-ins to enhance your browser, or utilities to help you spring clean your hard drive. There are whole web sites devoted to software, much of which you can try out before parting with your cash.
- **Music and sound**   Listening to radio stations from the other side of the world is possible on the Web, or you could download music to play on your PC. Some pages will have sound files which will allow you to hear a famous speech or a clip of the latest popular hit.
- **Images**   The Web is like a giant gallery where you can view photographs on just about any subject, drawings and paintings of the famous Masters in virtual art galleries, maps and diagrams illustrating the world, both ancient and modern, and computer-generated graphics similar to those used in games.
- **E-commerce**   You can buy a whole range of goods and services – a shopping arcade in your own home. You can buy your next car, arrange the insurance, check your bank balance, and order the parts to keep it going, not to mention the tools you might need to replace them. From booking your holiday to auctioning the souvenirs you've brought back but don't want, the possibilities for e-commerce are growing all the time.

E-mail

Electronic mail, or **e-mail** as it is more usually known, is used by people across the world to keep in touch, carry out business, and exchange files and information. Hundreds of millions of messages are exchanged every day, proving, perhaps, that the art of writing isn't yet dead! Compared to the normal postal system, or 'snail mail' as it is often called, e-mail is almost instantaneous and can be cheaper, with just the cost of a local phone call to send your message anywhere in the world. E-mail messages are sent via your ISP's mail server to your recipients' ISPs' mail servers, waiting until they next log on to collect their mail. Using e-mail you can send text messages and attach files which could be images, word-processed documents, sound or video clips, and even programs, directly from your computer to your recipient's computer for them to view and, perhaps, edit.

Newsgroups

One of the oldest parts of the Internet is **Usenet**, an online discussion community invented by three American graduates in 1979 to enable them to swap research material. This service of the Internet goes by different names, including **newsgroups**, electronic bulletin boards (EBS), discussion groups, and discussion forums. To be able to join this community you will need newsreading software on your computer, although this is already included in Microsoft's Outlook Express and Netscape Messenger. It's very much like sending an e-mail, but to a public mail box where anyone can 'post' a comment and anyone else can read it and send a reply. One word of warning, it's a public forum, so don't post anything remotely private!

A newsgroup will allow you to join in a discussion on just about any subject. Each newsgroup will deal with a different topic and you can post messages to the newsgroup expressing your views or asking for advice. To join a newsgroup you will need to subscribe, but this can be done through your ISP using Outlook Express, or most e-mail programs.

Understanding newsgroup names

Newsgroup addresses are different to web addresses (URLs, such as http://www.bbc.co.uk) or e-mail addresses (such as josie@heinemann.co.uk), and look like the example shown below:

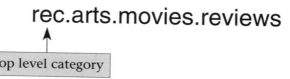

Newsgroups are organised in a hierarchy with each part of the address (from left to right) narrowing the scope of the group. The top level category, 'rec', has a large number of groups, using 'arts' helps to narrow the scope, and this is further narrowed by 'movies' and finally by 'reviews'.

Newsgroup addresses have developed over time with the first users setting the basic structure. Some of the top level categories are:

comp   computer-related subjects
rec   recreational subjects, such as hobbies, sports, arts and music
sci   sciences, usually the 'hard' sciences like biology and physics
soc   social issues, which could include societies and cultures
misc   miscellaneous, which could be anything as the name suggests, such as job searches, items for sale, etc.
alt   alternative subjects. This covers practically every other subject under the sun, including some of the more controversial or distasteful ones.

As countries have developed their own forums so the country code has been added. For example, uk.rec.gardening.misc would be a forum where UK gardeners might subscribe in order to exchange information and seek advice.

Talk and chat

While e-mail may be a great way of sending messages to family and friends, you have to wait for them to reply and a conversation isn't really possible. With Internet **chat** it is possible to have a 'conversation' in real time using text messages. Simply type in your message and your online friend will see it immediately and can respond straight away.

To start chatting, you usually join a public chat 'room' in which many people are talking (well, typing really!), but if you want a private chat you can go to a quieter 'room' away from the general hubbub of the public area.

Talk is very similar to chat, a 'conversation' in real time, but the method of connection is different. A talk program is used, and usually the conversation is between two people, rather than a crowd. Using the program, you can enter the e-mail address of the person to whom you want to talk and, if they are online (and want to talk to you!), you can begin your conversation. Despite being called 'talk', conversations are held in text, although some talk programs are including **voice chat** which will allow you to use a microphone to speak to someone, as long as they have speakers to hear you, of course! More recently talk goes under the name of **Instant Messaging**, and two of the better known programs for this are MSN Messenger (Windows 98) or Windows Messenger (Windows ME) (www. msn.co.uk) and AOL Instant Messenger (AIM) (www.aol.co.uk/aim). As these programs are proprietary, you and your contact have to have the same program running to be able to talk. This is set to change soon and you should be able to use any of these programs to communicate in the future.

> ## Information
>
> In Windows 98 Operating System, the instant messaging program is called MSN Messenger; in Windows ME Operating System, it is called Windows Messenger.

There are two types of chat: web-based chat and Internet chat. Web sites will host chat rooms and you can log on to them and sign in to join in the discussion going on. Many ISPs will provide systems to facilitate web-based chat, such as Freeserve Chat (www.freeserve.com/chat) and Yahoo! Chat (www.yahoo.co.uk/chat), which have dedicated web sites. Internet chat involves downloading a special chat program, such as mIRC (www.mirc.com), to communicate. These programs can require slightly more setting up before you use them, but are very popular.

One other form of communicating on the Net is using **Internet Telephony**, also known as **Voice over the Net (VON)**. Just like a normal phone, you can call someone, anywhere in the world, and hold a conversation, as long as you have a sound card, a microphone and speakers (or headset) on your computer (and they are online to receive your call). Add a web camera (web cam) and you could see the person you are talking to as well. Internet telephony allows you to talk to someone in Australia for the cost of a local phone call. You will need special software to use this facility, but Microsoft include their own VON, called **NetMeeting**, which is installed with Windows and Internet Explorer.

FTP

FTP (File Transfer Protocol) is the system used for transferring files across the Internet. FTP was used for uploading and downloading files long before the Web came into being, and is still the protocol used whenever you click on a link on a web page to download a file to your computer, it's just well hidden by the browser interface. FTP sites are huge libraries of files, some of which you will need a password to enter, others are open for everyone and are referred to as **anonymous ftp**, where you simply type in 'anonymous' and your e-mail address to gain access to the files. If you plan to build your own web site you will need some FTP software to upload your files to your ISP's web server.

FTP software has another advantage. If you are in the middle of downloading a file and your connection to your ISP is suddenly broken, you can reconnect and carry on with the download exactly where you left off.

Programs designed to connect to FTP servers are called FTP client programs, and there are both freeware and shareware ones available on the Net for download, for example WS_FTP (www.ipswitch.com) and Cute FTP (www.cuteftp.com).

Telnet

If you want to access a remote computer, you may need to use **Telnet**. Like FTP, Telnet predates the Web by many years, and doesn't have the friendly GUI (Graphic User Interface) that we know from our browsers, but it does still allow access to information systems, such as library book catalogues. One of the most popular uses for Telnet is to play MUD (Multi-User Dungeon) games, which are like text adventures games where you can interact with other players.

When you access a remote computer, you have to follow the rules set up by the system administrator, which may well be different for each computer you connect to. For this reason, there is no single Telnet program which can be used. Windows does include a basic Telnet program which can be accessed by clicking on the **Start** button and selecting **Run** from the pop-up menu. Enter 'telnet' in the **Open** box and click on **OK**.

E-commerce

You can buy an amazing variety of things on the Web, such as books, CDs, computer equipment, holidays, groceries; in fact the list is endless. This is called **electronic commerce** or **e-commerce** and is a way of doing business online.

Many companies will advertise on the Web, and provide links to their lists of items for sale so that you can quickly find what you want. You can pay for your goods electronically by entering your credit or debit card details. The pages where you would enter such sensitive information usually have special security features so that your information can't be misused.

The following screen shots show how you could buy the latest CD release by your favourite band on the Web.

Add this CD to your virtual shopping basket and then proceed to payment – just like a supermarket

Click on this link to find out more about the CD

Figure 2.1 Buying on the Web

The advantages of e-commerce are:

- People who live in country areas can buy goods which are only available in stores in large cities.
- People with disabilities, or who are elderly, can buy goods without leaving their home.
- Less trips to towns and shopping centres could mean less traffic congestion and less pollution.
- Shopping is quick and easy, with goods being delivered to your door, generating more jobs in delivery firms.

The disadvantages of e-commerce are:

- People could feel isolated and cut off without trips to shops where they meet other people.
- Walking round the shops is exercise, whereas buying your goods from home means less exercise which could lead to health problems.
- It could be seen as slightly risky giving out your credit card details over the Internet. Exchanging goods could be difficult.
- You can't 'try before you buy' when you buy goods over the Internet.
- There could be fewer shops, especially locally, which means that people without computers may not be able to get the goods they need.

Audio/video conferencing

Audio conferencing is a way that people in many different parts of the country or the world can talk to each other without leaving their home or office. Add a web camera (web cam) and you can see them too (as long as they also have web cams). Many businesses and educational establishments use this facility to conduct meetings and teaching sessions. The big advantage of audio/video conferencing is that people don't need to spend many hours travelling to venues across the country to attend meetings, which can therefore save time and cost. By using the links, data and documents can be sent to other participants electronically, giving people the opportunity to have discussions and debates while avoiding the time it takes sending documents by snail mail.

Audio/video conferencing programs will often have a whiteboard facility. This allows participants in the meeting to draw diagrams or pictures which everyone can see and can edit in response to discussion. Completed drawings, etc. can be saved or printed.

To conduct video conferencing, you would need access to the Internet with a high-speed connection, as video is very resource hungry and a standard 56 K modem, like one used with many home computers, could make the images jerky and unclear. You would also need a web cam, speakers and sound card, microphone and the same conferencing program used by everyone in the meeting, such as Microsoft's NetMeeting, which is installed with the Windows operating system.

Data conferencing

To enhance the facilities in a video conference, it is also possible to share running programs so that data can be edited by other members at the meeting. Using NetMeeting, for example, a Word file can be opened on your own computer and shared with others at the conference. Control of the program can be passed to them and data can be edited collaboratively. A high-speed connection, such as ISDN, would be preferable for everyone participating in the meeting; otherwise it could take some time for the windows to be displayed on everyone's computer screen.

Desktop sharing

Desktop sharing allows you to manage another computer from your own computer. This will allow you to use the other computer as if you were sitting at it in person. For example, you can call up your computer at work from your computer at home and access your files on the work machine. This is a great advantage if you travel or need to use the resources of the other machine. During the period you are accessing your work machine, you would need to password protect it to prevent anyone else using it at the same time.

→ **Check your knowledge 1**

1 What language is used to write web pages?
2 What might web pages contain?
3 What is the difference between newsgroups and chat?
4 What is the difference between web-based chat and Internet chat?
5 What is FTP, and why is it used?
6 What type of software would you need to upload a web page?
7 Why might video/audio conferencing be used?
8 Why would a high-speed Internet connection be better for a video conference?
9 What does data conferencing allow you to do?
10 List three advantages and three disadvantages of e-commerce.

Using search engines

There is such a huge amount of information on the Web that finding the bit you particularly want can seem a hit or miss affair. This is where **search engines**, **directories** and **meta search sites** can be a real boon. Finding something using a search engine can range from simply entering a keyword and clicking 'Go' to more complex criteria to narrow the search. There are many search engines available, and the best way of finding out which one suits you is to try a few. It's a good idea to add your search engines to your **Favorites** folder so you can choose the best one for any particular search as they all have their strengths and weaknesses. To search the Web, you can use straightforward search engines, or directories, which have a hierarchical structure, listing pages grouped by themes, or mixed search tools which have both. Meta search sites submit your query to several search engines at the same time, and can be a useful tool to use for some purposes.

Some of the popular search engines and directories are:

AltaVista	www.uk.altavista.com	Looksmart	www.looksmart.com
Excite	www.excite.co.uk	Yahoo!	www.yahoo.com
HotBot	www.hotbot.com	UK Online	www.ukonline.co.uk
Lycos UK	www.lycos.co.uk	What's New	www.whatsnew.com
Google	www.google.com		

Some meta search sites are:

Dogpile	www.dogpile.com
Metacrawler	www.metacrawler.com
Copernic	www.copernic.com

Last, but not least, is Ask Jeeves (www.ask.co.uk), where you can enter a question and pick the most likely similar question from the list of questions that Jeeves knows the answer to.

To use search engines, there are several ways to enter your words in a search box.

Basic search techniques

- Type in a keyword or words. Be warned – this may produce many thousands of 'hits' which could take forever to go through to find what you want. For example, entering *paper airplanes* will bring up 204,000 hits because the search engine may list all pages with either *paper* or *airplanes* in them.

Figure 2.2 A search engine

- Enclosing your keywords in quote marks can help narrow the search as the search engine will look for pages containing both words. For example, entering *"paper airplanes"* will bring up fewer pages, 27,200, however still a lot to go through.

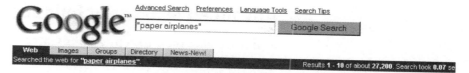

Figure 2.3 Using quote marks to search

- Ordering your keywords in descending order of importance can help.
- Using + and − signs allows you to be much more specific, as the word which comes after the + sign must be included and the word which comes after the − sign must be excluded. For example, if you wanted pages for paper airplanes which mentioned gliders specifically, you would use *"paper airplanes" + gliders* in your search to give a mere 1400 hits.

Figure 2.4 Using quote marks and plus sign to search

Whereas *"paper airplanes" − gliders* would give you 25,800 hits which would be all the pages containing 'paper airplanes' as a keyword where 'gliders' wasn't mentioned specifically.

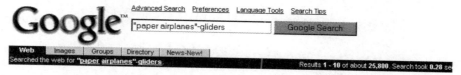

Figure 2.5 Using quote marks and minus sign to search

Different search engines will have other tricks for refining your search. For example, in Yahoo! you can add a **t:** in front of the keywords to get a search on just the title of the page.

With some search engines, you can also use **wildcards** in your search. Using the ***** (asterisk) to stand for something you can't specify will broaden your search – useful if you can't remember how to spell a word.

Most search sites will have a **Help** button which will give you some tips on searching as shown in the screen capture from the Google search site.

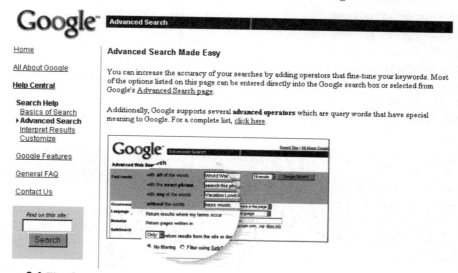

Figure 2.6 Tips for searching

Advanced search techniques

It may be necessary to refine your search and to use an advanced search. Advanced searches use Boolean operators, which are words like AND, OR, NOT, AND NOT, NEAR and brackets ().

- **AND** finds all pages with the specified words or phrases. For example, *paper AND planes* would find all documents with both the word *paper* and the word *planes*.
- **AND NOT** excludes pages containing the specified word or phrase. For example, *planes AND NOT paper* would find documents with the word *planes* but not with the word *paper*.
- **OR** finds pages with at least one of the words or phrases. For example, *paper OR planes* would find documents with either the word *paper* or the word *plane*. It may also find pages which contain both words too.

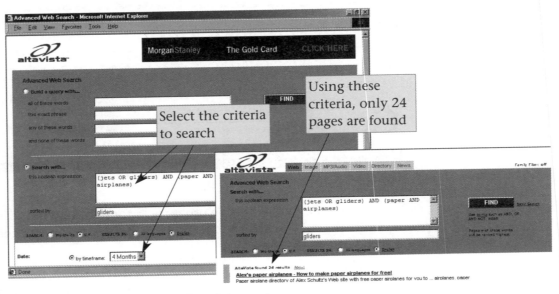

Figure 2.7 Using timescale and position of words to search

Note:

Different search engines will use slightly different criteria. It's worth getting to know the ones to use for your favourite search engines by looking at their Search Help.

- **( )** (brackets) are used to group words together. For example, *(jets OR gliders) AND (paper AND airplanes)* finds pages with *jets and paper airplanes* as well as pages with *gliders and paper airplanes*.

You can further refine your search by entering a timescale, for example pages less than 4 months old, or pages only in English. On the AltaVista search shown you can also have the hits sorted with *gliders* at the top of the list.

Try it out!

Use some of the search techniques to find web pages on the space shuttle and compare the number of hits you get.

Navigating web pages

Having used your search engine and found a list of relevant web sites, you can then begin to navigate the web pages to find one that is of particular interest.

Using links

Many web pages will have a mix of text and images on them. Some of the text may have lines underneath and some of the images may change or move as you pass your mouse pointer over them. These are **hyperlinks** (also called **hotspots**) which are used to link to other pages. Your mouse pointer will change to a hand with a pointing finger 🖑 as you move it over the hyperlinks. If you click on one of these links you will find another page opens. Following hyperlinks in this way can lead you from your own computer to a page halfway across the world. Hotspots on web pages can lead you anywhere!

Hyperlinks don't just open other web pages, they could play a video clip or a sound file, download an application, run a program, show a picture. You have to click on them to find out what happens.

On a web page you may find:

- **Plain text**   This is ordinary text. Clicking on this will do nothing at all!
- **Hypertext link**   A text link to another page which could be on the same web site or on another computer anywhere in the world. Hypertext links are nearly always underlined, although they can be in any font or colour.
- **Image**   A picture or graphic that makes the web site look interesting and colourful. Although an image might be useful to illustrate something, clicking on it won't take you anywhere.
- **Hyperlinked image**   Clicking on this link will open a new page. It probably won't look any different to any other image, but don't forget that your mouse pointer will change to a hand when you pass it over a hyperlinked image.
- **Image map**   This is an image made up of smaller images, such as a map of Britain, where different parts of the map will take you to information about each county.
- **E-mail link**   You can use this link to open your e-mail program and send a message to the address automatically placed in the Address box.

Note:

A web site can be made up of just one page – perhaps just some information and a few pictures – or hundreds of pages such as a company might have, showing you all their products.

Information

You can imagine that all this clicking on hyperlinks can take you a long way from home, and you may find that you've suddenly become lost. The **toolbar** in Explorer is your way home – literally. Clicking on the **Home** button on the toolbar will take you back to where you began – your homepage.

If we follow the links from our search for paper airplanes we can navigate to a web page which will give us instructions on how to make a model paper airplane, as in Figure 2.8.

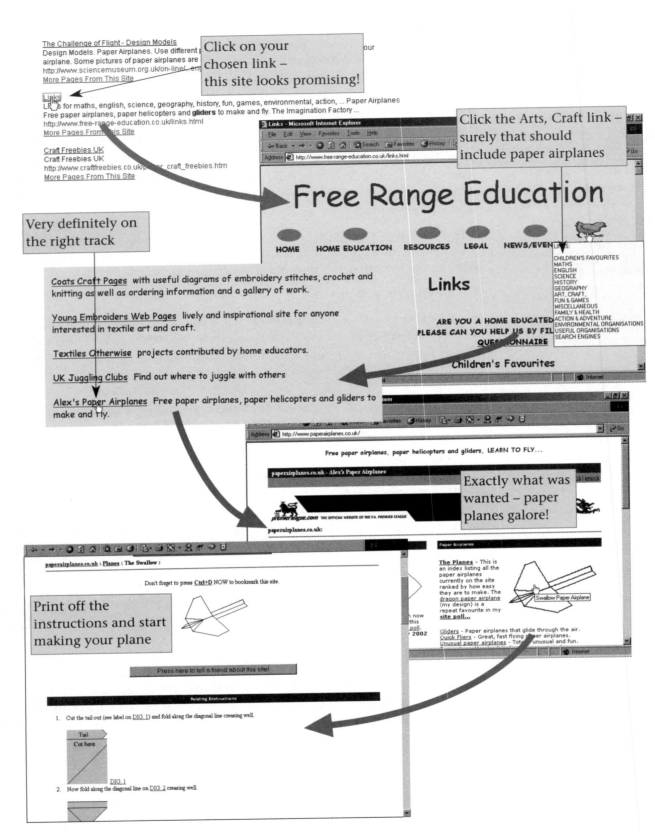

The Challenge of Flight - Design Models
Design Models. Paper Airplanes. Use different ... our
airplane. Some pictures of paper airplanes are ...
http://www.sciencemuseum.org.uk/on-line/... em...
More Pages From This Site

Links
Links for maths, english, science, geography, history, fun, games, environmental, action, ... Paper Airplanes
Free paper airplanes, paper helicopters and **gliders** to make and fly. The Imagination Factory ...
http://www.free-range-education.co.uk/links.html
More Pages From This Site

Craft Freebies UK
Craft Freebies UK
http://www.craftfreebies.co.uk/paper_craft_freebies.htm
More Pages From This Site

Click on your
chosen link –
this site looks promising!

Click the Arts, Craft link –
surely that should
include paper airplanes

Free Range Education

HOME   HOME EDUCATION   RESOURCES   LEGAL   NEWS/EVENTS

LINKS:
CHILDREN'S FAVOURITES
MATHS
ENGLISH
SCIENCE
HISTORY
GEOGRAPHY
ART, CRAFT,
FUN & GAMES
MISCELLANEOUS
FAMILY & HEALTH
ACTION & ADVENTURE
ENVIRONMENTAL ORGANISATIONS
USEFUL ORGANISATIONS
SEARCH ENGINES

Links

ARE YOU A HOME EDUCATED
PLEASE CAN YOU HELP US BY FIL...
QUESTIONNAIRE

Children's Favourites

Very definitely on
the right track

Coats Craft Pages with useful diagrams of embroidery stitches, crochet and
knitting as well as ordering information and a gallery of work.

Young Embroiders Web Pages lively and inspirational site for anyone
interested in textile art and craft.

Textiles Otherwise projects contributed by home educators.

UK Juggling Clubs Find out where to juggle with others

Alex's Paper Airplanes Free paper airplanes, paper helicopters and gliders to
make and fly.

Free paper airplanes, paper helicopters and gliders, LEARN TO FLY...

paperairplanes.co.uk - Alex's Paper Airplanes

premierleague.com THE OFFICIAL WEBSITE OF THE F.A. PREMIER LEAGUE

paperairplanes.co.uk:

Exactly what was
wanted – paper
planes galore!

Paper Airplanes

The Planes - This is
an index listing all the
paper airplanes
currently on the site
ranked by how easy
they are to make. The
dragon paper airplane
(my design) is a
repeat favourite in my
site poll...

Swallow Paper Airplane

Gliders - Paper airplanes that glide through the air.
Quick Fliers - Great, fast flying paper airplanes.
Unusual paper airplanes - Tota... unusual and fun.

paperairplanes.co.uk : Planes : The Swallow :

Don't forget to press **Ctrl+D** NOW to bookmark this site.

Print off the
instructions and start
making your plane

Press here to tell a friend about this site!

Folding Instructions

1.   Cut the tail out (see label on DIG. 1) and fold along the diagonal line creasing well.

Tail
Cut here

DIG. 1
2.   Now fold along the diagonal line on DIG. 2 creasing well.

Figure 2.8 Following links

Remember:

A **Universal Resource Locator (URL)** is the Internet address of a particular web page. These addresses begin with **http://** followed by **www** to indicate that it's a page on the World Wide Web.

Using URLs

If you know the URL of the web page, it is a straightforward task to find the information you want.

Task 2.1	Loading a web page knowing the URL of the page you want to view

Method

1   Click in the browser's **Address** bar.
2   Enter the URL of the web page you want to view.
3   Press the **Enter** key on the keyboard.

Hint:

If you have entered a URL in the Address bar, you can also click the **Go** button
Go to the right of the Address bar to go to the web page.

Using your Favorites folder

If you save the web addresses of the pages you often visit, or know you might want to visit again, in your Favorites (American spelling!) folder, you can go back to them with the click of a button.

Task 2.2	Loading page from Favorites folder

Method

1   Load your browser and connect to your ISP.
2   Click on the **Favorites** button on the toolbar.
3   Select folder and then the address for the web page you want from the list. The web page will load.
4   To close the Favorites pane, click on the **Favorites** button on the toolbar again.
5   Disconnect and close your browser when you have finished.

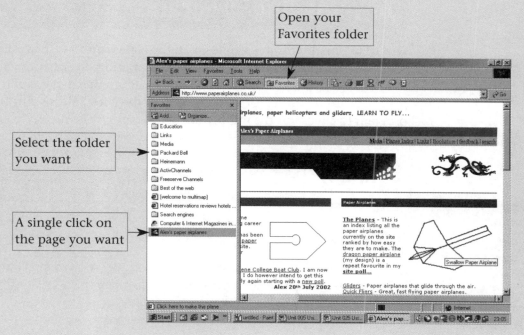

Open your Favorites folder

Select the folder you want

A single click on the page you want

Figure 2.9 Accessing a page from Favorites

→ Practise your skills 1

1 Create a folder in your **Favorites** and name it **Search Engines**.
2 Select five of the search engines and load the web pages.
3 Add the URLs to your Search Engines folder in your Favorites.
4 Select two search engines from your Favorites and load each one in turn to search for the following using a range of search techniques:

   a York University   **b** Video conferencing   **c** Mountain bikes

   List and compare the numbers of hits for each search engine.
5 Use your word processing program to write a brief report on your research and make a recommendation about the best search engine to use.

→ Practise your skills 2

1 Open your word processing program and start a new document.
2 Load each of the search engines in turn from your Favorites folder and access the Search Help for each one.
3 Copy the information about using advanced searches and paste it into your open document.
4 Save your document as **search techniques** and print out a copy for future reference.

→ Check your knowledge 2

1 What is the difference between a meta search site and a search engine?
2 Name two of the Boolean operators you might use in an advanced search.
3 How can you tell if something is a hyperlink on a web page?
4 How would you get back to your homepage?
5 What is a URL?

Downloading programs

One of the many reasons people go on the Net is to access the vast store of software available. You may want a particular utility to enhance your browsing, anti-virus software to keep your computer safe, an updated driver for your graphics card or printer, or a trial version of the latest release of your favourite program to check out the improvements. Whatever the reason, you'll need to download the program to your computer before you can begin to use it.

Task 2.3 — Downloading a program

Note:

Because of the risk of viruses being transmitted from a downloaded file, you should always use your virus checker to make sure the file is clear before you open it.

Method

1 Click on the **download** link (usually similar to a hyperlink or a button).
2 Select the **Save this program to disk** option.
3 Click on **OK**.
4 Choose where you want to save the file on your hard drive and click on **Save**.

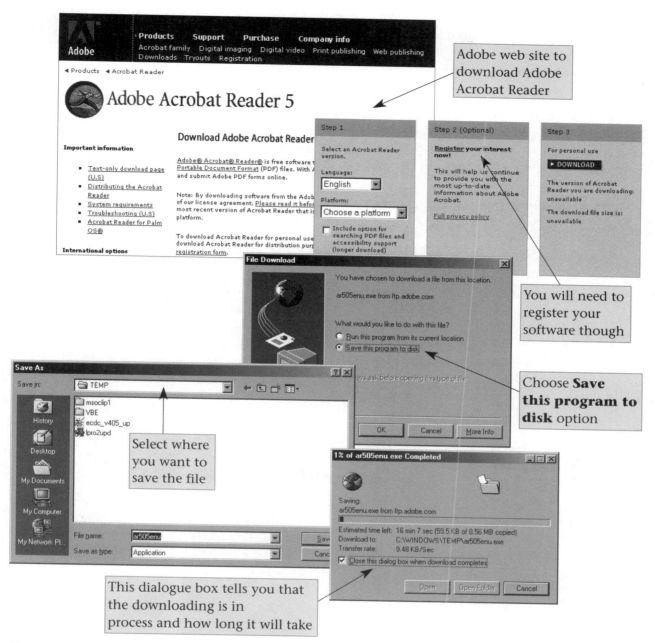

Figure 2.10 Downloading a file

Information

If you select **Run this program from its current location** it will open the file to view or play straightaway (as long as you have the appropriate program loaded onto your computer). This will not download the program or file onto your hard drive.

Information

If you have downloaded a program, such as Acrobat Reader®, you will then have to install it onto your computer. If you have downloaded a file, such as a video clip, you will have to load the appropriate application and open the file.

Method

1 Read and note down the instructions for installing the program from the web site.
2 Locate the saved file on your hard drive.
3 Follow the instructions from your notes – often this will be to double click on the .exe file.
4 Follow the onscreen instructions to install your program.

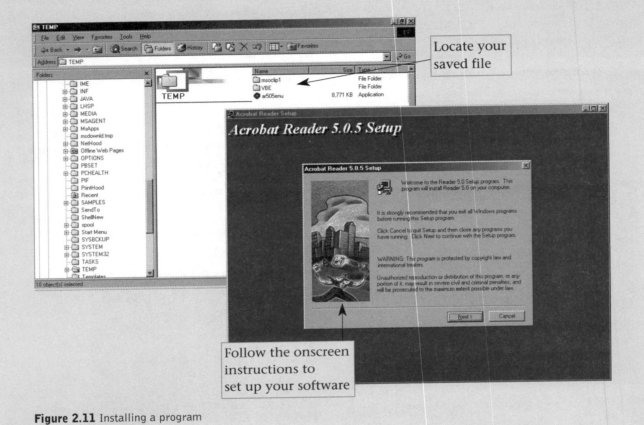

Locate your saved file

Follow the onscreen instructions to set up your software

Figure 2.11 Installing a program

Note:

Downloading and installing a shareware program (WinZip) was covered in Section 1.

Using FTP software

Hidden behind your browser interface is the File Transfer Protocol (FTP) used to download your files, but FTP can also give you access to more than just the files on the Web. There are two ways of accessing files using FTP. One is through your browser, the other is via a dedicated FTP program.

The Gutenberg Project aims to publish many books, especially classics such as *Alice in Wonderland*, as etexts which you can download to your computer and either read onscreen or print out to read later. The etexts are available on this site: ftp://ftp.mirror.ac.uk/sites/metalab.unc.edu/pub/docs/books/gutenberg/.

Method

1   Load your browser.

2   Enter the URL of the FTP site in the **Address** box (ftp://ftp.mirror.ac.uk/sites/metalab.unc.edu/pub/
    docs/books/gutenberg/ in the example shown).

    Note: The address will start with **ftp** not the usual **http**.

3   Scroll down and select a file or directory which may provide the information you are looking for.
    Look for a file with 'INDEX', 'README', or 'DIRECTORY', which may give you more information
    about the contents of the site.

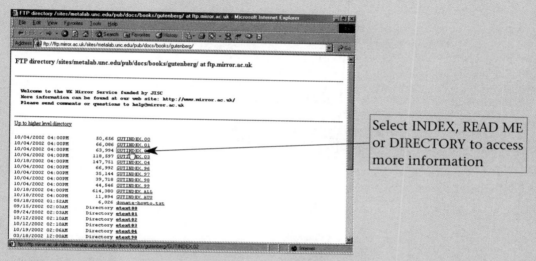

Figure 2.12 Selecting a directory

4   Click on the link and read the file carefully – this one gives clear instructions on finding the etext for
    Alice in Wonderland.

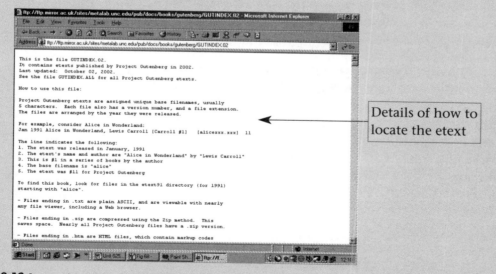

Figure 2.13 Instructions are provided for finding an etext

5   Select the file you need.

6   Right click on the file and select the **Save Target As** option from the pop-up menu.

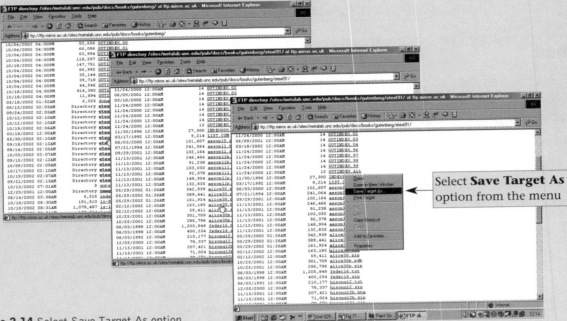

Select **Save Target As** option from the menu

Figure 2.14 Select Save Target As option

7   Browse your hard drive and select a location to save your file.

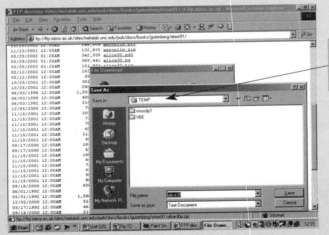

Browse your hard drive to select the location to save your file

Figure 2.15 Select location to save file

8   Browse your hard drive to find the saved file and open it in the appropriate program (you could do this by double clicking on the file).

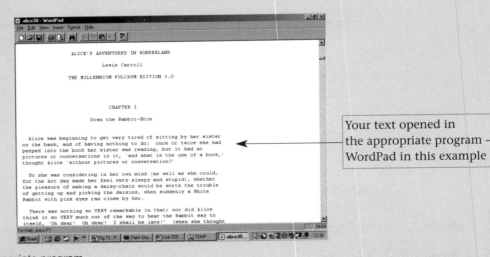

Your text opened in the appropriate program – WordPad in this example

Figure 2.16 Open file in appropriate program

Task 2.6   Using an FTP program to access ftp files

Method

I   Connect to your ISP.

2   Download an FTP program to your computer and install it.

3   Start the FTP program by selecting it from the **Start/Programs** menu. This example will use CuteFTP.

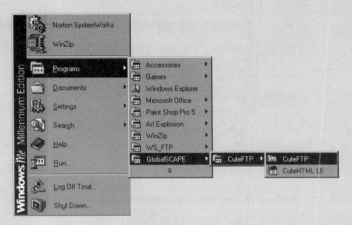

Figure 2.17 Selecting FTP program

4   Select **Site Manager** from the File menu. Click the **New** button and enter the details of the ftp site you wish to access in the dialogue box. In this example the Gutenberg site is on the ftp.mirror.ac.uk site. As this is an anonymous ftp site, there is no need to fill the **FTP site User Name** or **Password** boxes.

5   Click **Connect** to go to the site.

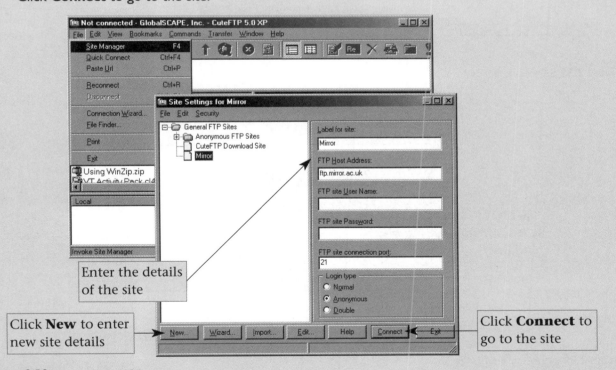

Figure 2.18 Connecting to ISP

6   When connection is confirmed, you can browse the directories in the right-hand pane.

7   Select the file you want to transfer and click the **Transfer** arrow or select **Download** from the
Transfer menu.

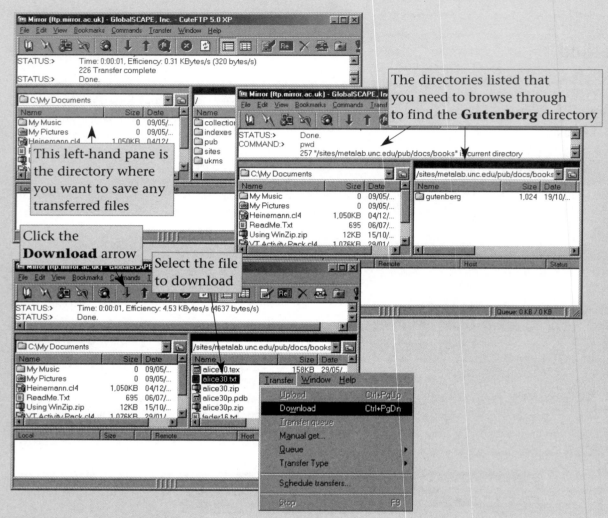

The directories listed that
you need to browse through
to find the **Gutenberg** directory

This left-hand pane is
the directory where
you want to save any
transferred files

Click the
Download arrow

Select the file
to download

Figure 2.19 Select file and download

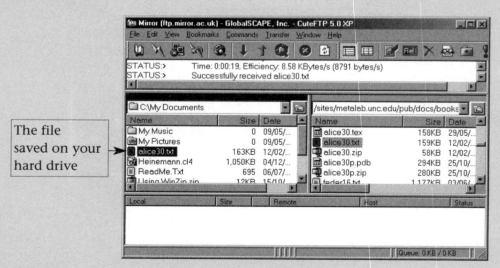

The file
saved on your
hard drive

Figure 2.20 Accessing the ftp file

8   Access and load the file from your hard dive.

→ Practise your skills 3

1 Connect to the Internet and search for an appropriate FTP program.
2 Download the program and save to your hard drive.
3 Install the program.
4 Load the FTP software and locate an anonymous ftp site which will allow you to download music onto your computer (ftp.cs.ruu.nl. is one example).
5 Select one of the pieces of music to download and play on your computer.
6 Close your connection to the FTP site and to the Internet.
7 Locate and play the piece of music selected.

Participating in a newsgroup

You can find information, advice or just plain gossip from others in a newsgroup. Both Outlook Express and Netscape Messenger have facilities to access newsgroups.

Task 2.7　Subscribing to a newsgroup

Method

1 Load your e-mail program (Outlook Express in this example) and click on the **Set up a Newsgroups account**.

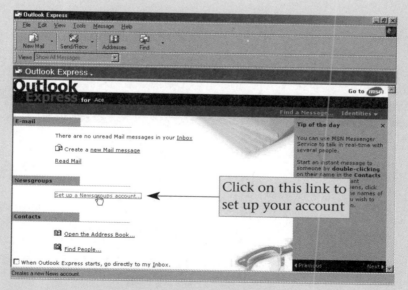

Figure 2.21 Setting up a Newsgroups account

2 Follow the steps in the **Internet Connection Wizard**, which will include your name, e-mail address and your ISP's news server address (this will be something like news.supersurfer.net). You will receive a message telling you that you have successfully set up your account. Click on **Finish** to save the settings.

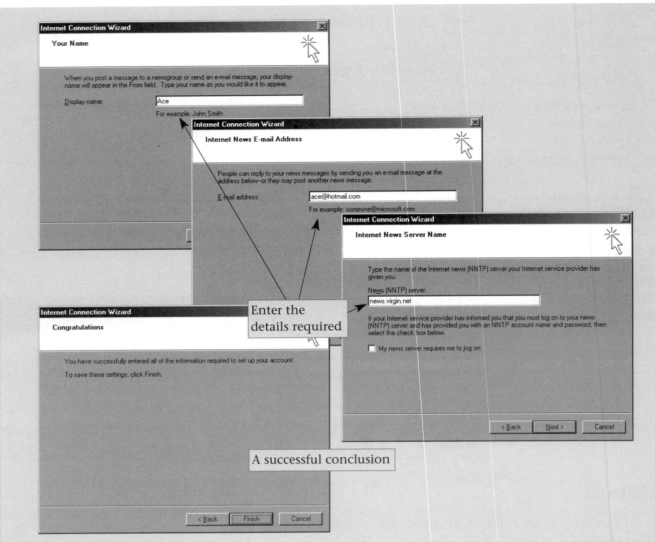

Enter the
details required

A successful conclusion

Figure 2.22 Using Internet Connection Wizard

3 In the dialogue box which appears, click on **Yes** to download the newsgroups. You may be prompted to connect to your ISP if you are not already connected. The downloading can take a few minutes, but you only need to do it once.

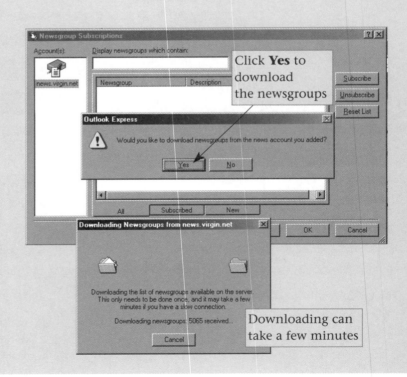

Click **Yes** to download the newsgroups

Downloading can take a few minutes

4 Scroll down the list of newsgroups until you find one you would like to subscribe to, select it and click on **Subscribe**. A small icon appears 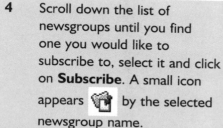 by the selected newsgroup name.

5 Click on **Go to** button to obtain a list of all the postings for the newsgroup selected, and they will be shown in the right hand pane of Outlook Express.

Figure 2.23 Downloading the newsgroup

Your selected newsgroup

Click the **Subscribe** button

Click the **Go to** button to access the postings

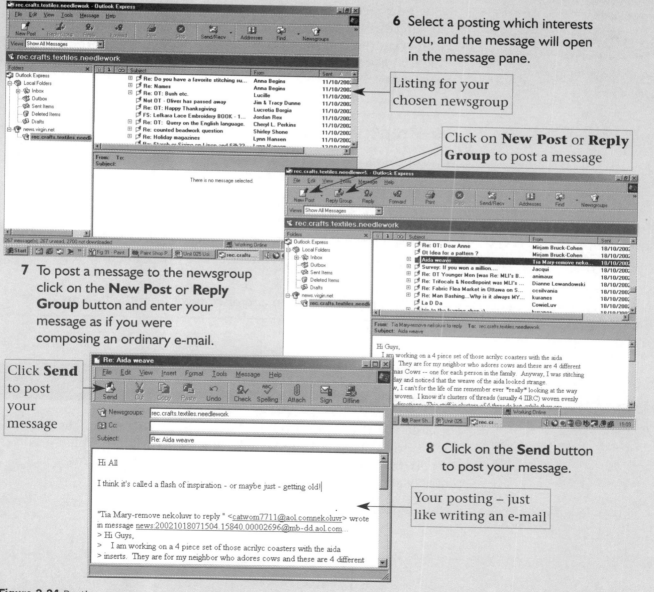

6 Select a posting which interests you, and the message will open in the message pane.

Listing for your chosen newsgroup

Click on **New Post** or **Reply Group** to post a message

7 To post a message to the newsgroup click on the **New Post** or **Reply Group** button and enter your message as if you were composing an ordinary e-mail.

Click **Send** to post your message

8 Click on the **Send** button to post your message.

Your posting – just like writing an e-mail

Figure 2.24 Posting a message

Netiquette

Although there are no rules or regulations on the Net, and that includes newsgroups too, there are informal rules which you should observe, commonly known as **Netiquette.**

- TYPING MESSAGES IN CAPITALS IS SEEN AS SHOUTING AND CONSIDERED IMPOLITE.
- Don't write insults to others or be rude about their opinions. This is called **Flaming** and can result in a flurry of ever-increasing strident messages. This is sometimes referred to as Flame Wars, and won't make you many friends in the newsgroup!
- Don't add lengthy signatures to your postings – it can increase download times and not make you very popular!
- For the same reason, don't include all the previous message in your reply – just a line or two to give a general indication of the content will do.
- Read a few of the postings on the newsgroup to get an idea of the thread of the postings. It is a good idea to check the **FAQ** (Frequently Asked Questions) file before you begin – it may help to answer your question if it's already been posted by 'newbies' several times already!
- Don't post the same message to several newsgroups, especially if it only vaguely relates to the topic. This is called cross-posting, and isn't very popular.

→ Practise your skills 4

1 Connect to the Internet and load your e-mail program (it will need to support newsgroups).
2 Set up your subscription to the news server.
3 Download the newsgroups.
4 Select a newsgroup that interests you and subscribe to it.
5 Obtain a list of postings and select one which interests you.
6 Print out a copy of the message.
7 Exit your e-mail program and disconnect from the Internet.

Participating in a chat session

The easiest way to chat is to go into a web-based chat room. The example below is from http://chat.msn.co.uk, which is easy to use. You'll need a .Net passport, but if you have already got a Hotmail e-mail account, you'll probably already have one.

Method

1   Connect to your ISP and enter the URL of the chat room web site in your **Address** bar.

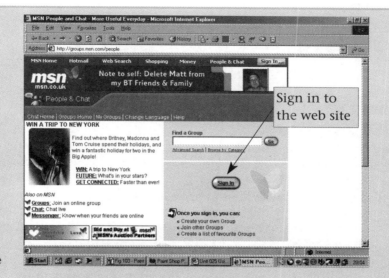

Figure 2.25 Signing in to a web site

2   When you sign in for the first time a chat tool will be automatically installed on your computer.

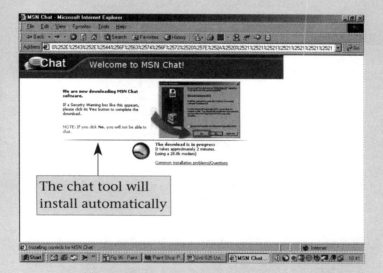

Figure 2.26 Automatic installation of chat tool

3   Select the chat room which appeals to you – there are several different topics to choose from, so there's something to interest everyone.

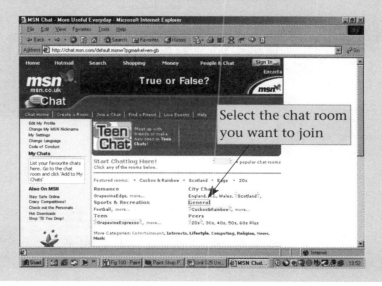

Figure 2.27 Select chat room

4 There are chat rooms for complete novices – such as this one, Beginners room for new MSN users.

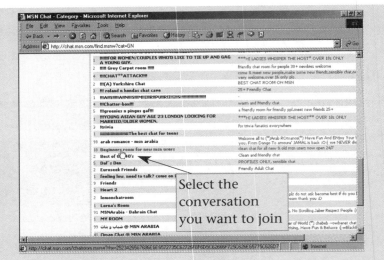

Figure 2.28 Select conversation

5 Sign into the chat room with your e-mail address and password.

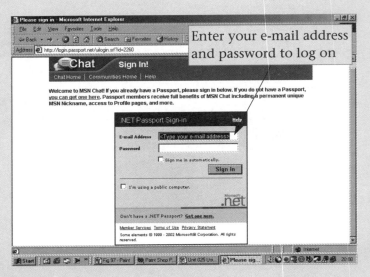

Figure 2.29 Signing in to chat room

6 Wait while you are connected to the server for the chat room you requested.

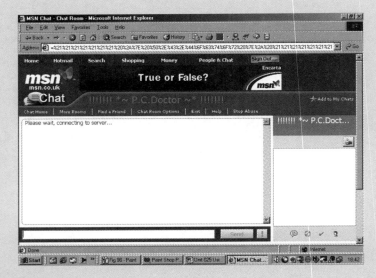

Figure 2.30 Connecting to chat room

7 Now you can begin to chat – simply enter your message in the text box and click on **Send**. You've joined the chat!

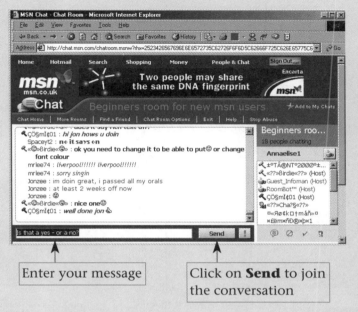

Figure 2.31 Joining the conversation

Instead of joining a chat room on a dedicated web site, you can also chat using **Internet Relay Chat (IRC)**. IRC is a system which enables Internet users to communicate in real time by entering text messages. It has been around since the Internet's early days in 1985. IRC tools can be downloaded from the Net onto your computer and, although slightly more technical than using a web site chat room, can offer more possibilities for chatting. One such shareware chat program is mIRC, which can be downloaded from www.mirc.co.uk.

Task 2.9 — Joining a chat room using mIRC

Method

1 Double click the **mIRC** icon ![mIRC icon] or select from the **Start/Programs** menu to load mIRC.

2 Close the splash screen using the Close Window icon (the cross) at the top right-hand corner of the window.

3 Enter the details in the **mIRC Options** dialogue box and select a server to connect to from the drop down list box. This example shows Random EU DALnet server.

4 Click the **Connect to IRC Server** button (you may need to be online for this or you may be prompted to connect to your ISP).

5 Select a **Channel** from the list displayed. There are many thousands of channels, but some of the most popular will be listed here. The **Newbies** channel (shown here) is a channel for beginners, so it is a good place to start.

6   The current conversation will be shown in the main window. To join the chat, enter your text in the text input box at the bottom of the window and press **Enter**. Your message will appear in the chat window.

7   Exit the chat by closing the window (it is polite to say goodbye, though!).

8   Close mIRC and disconnect.

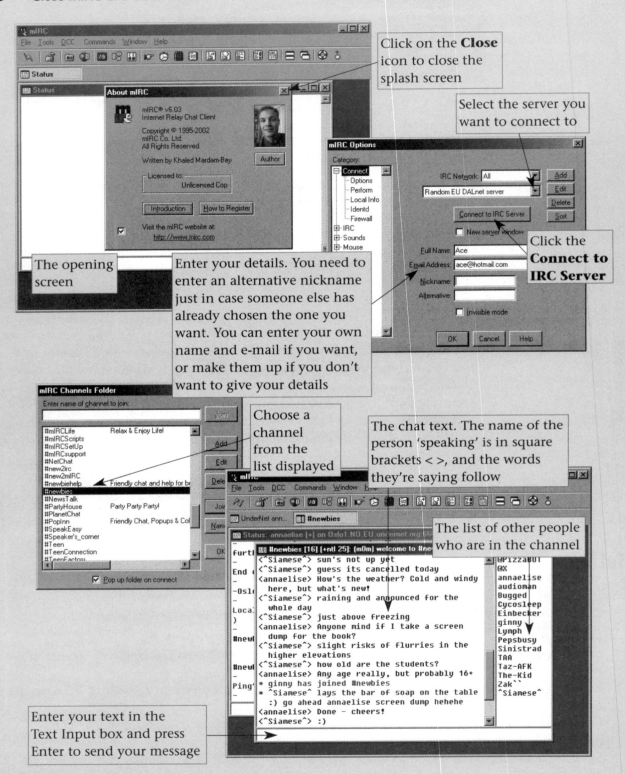

Figure 2.32 Joining a chat room using mIRC

Chat language

It can be time-consuming to type out your messages in full when you're chatting in real time, so a list of common abbreviations and symbols are used much like phone texting. Some of the common ones are:

AFAIK	As far as I know
AFK	Away from keyboard
A/S/L	Age/Sex/Location (ie how old are you, are you male or female, and where are you?)
BBIAB	Be back in a bit
BBL	Be back later
BFN	Bye for now
FYI	For your information
LOL	Laugh out loud
NP	No problem
TTYL	Talk to you later

There are many more and you may find them in the FAQ (Frequently Asked Questions) on the chat server, or on a web page.

Warning!

You should *never* give out personal details, such as your address or phone number, when using chat rooms. It would also be very unwise to arrange to meet someone you have only met in a chat room unless it was in a public place and you had a friend or another adult with you.

Information

People are often concerned about some of the topics in chat rooms, but if you stick to fairly straightforward channels you should be OK. Avoid channels with lots of Xs or Zs in their names as these might be dealing with less pleasant topics or pedalling pirated software.

Instant messaging

Live online chatting in a private group is known as **instant messaging**. To be able to join in the discussion, everyone needs to have the same software installed (and being used to chat) on their computers. There are several instant messaging programs, but unfortunately, at the moment, they are not compatible, although this may change in the not too distant future.

Some well-known instant messaging programs are Windows MSN Messenger (now called Windows Messenger), Yahoo! Messenger, ICQ (pronounced I seek you!) and AIM (AOL Instant Messenger). MSN Messenger is included in the Windows ME operating system and Windows Messenger is included with the Windows XP version, but for Windows 98 users it can be downloaded for free from the Microsoft web site.

Information

The following screen capture images and method show Windows ME as the operating system and MSN Messenger as the instant messaging program in use, although the procedures for many of the other programs will be similar. If you are using Windows XP and Windows Messenger, the screens will look slightly different, but the process will be much the same.

To use MSN Messenger or Windows Messenger, you will need to have a Hotmail account or a .Net Passport from www.passport.com (a passport from Microsoft which allows you log in to web sites that use the passport technology).

Instant messaging allows you to maintain a contact list, also known as a 'buddy list', of friends or contacts who use the same program, so whenever you connect to the Internet, you can see if they are online or not. If they are, and want to chat, you can exchange messages in real time – much more like holding a conversation.

Task 2.10 | Using Microsoft's instant messaging program

Method

1   If Messenger isn't installed on your computer, locate, download and install it from the Internet.
2   Load the Messenger program from the **Start/Programs/Accessories/Communications** menus.

Information

If you don't have a .Net Passport, the signup wizard will prompt you to sign up for one. If you do have a passport or a Hotmail account, click **Next**. If you haven't got either yet, follow the instructions to register for one.

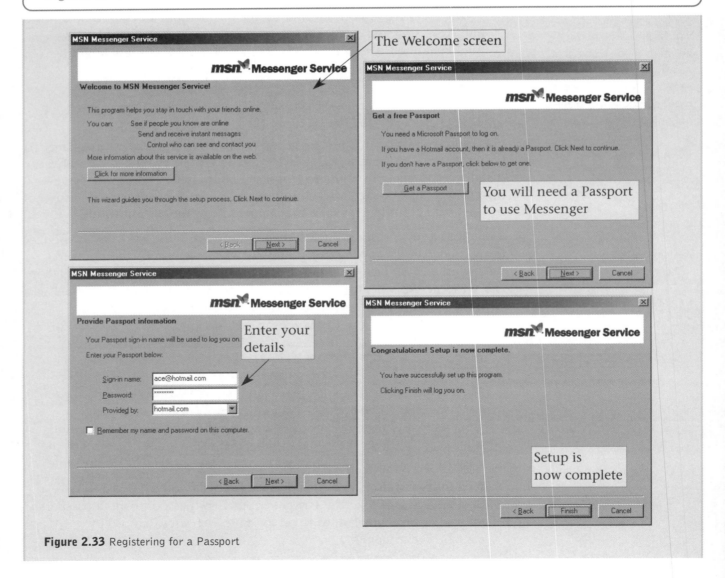

Figure 2.33 Registering for a Passport

3   When you have registered for your Passport, the Messenger window opens and, if you are not connected to the Internet, you will be prompted to sign in.

4   The next dialogue box will ask you to enter your e-mail address and your password. Click on **OK**. Once you have entered these details, Messenger will sign you into their service.

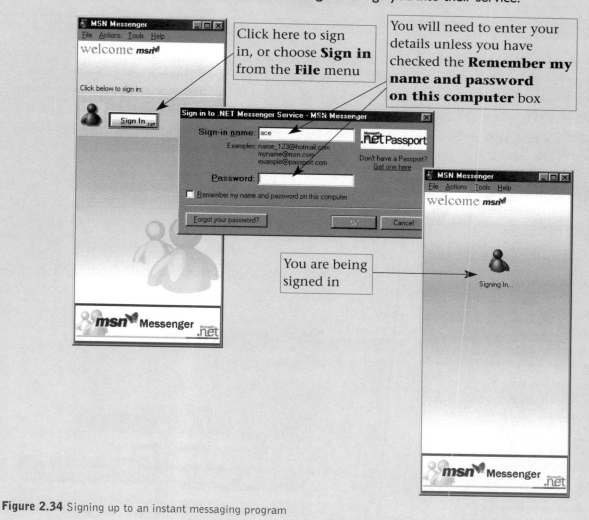

Figure 2.34 Signing up to an instant messaging program

Information

When you open your Messenger program in future, you will be able to log on using either the link in the Messenger window, or the **File/Sign In** option.

If you check the **Remember my name and password on this computer** box on the log in screen, you won't have to enter your details again.

MSN Messenger version 5 is shown in the screen capture images. If you are using an older version of MSN Messenger, you may receive this alert asking if you want to download a newer version. Select the option you want.

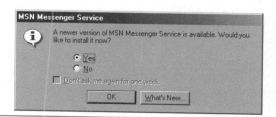

Figure 2.35 MSN Messenger

Having signed into the Instant Messenger service, you need to build your list of contacts.

5   Click the **Add** option in the list. In the dialogue box which appears, you are asked to select one of the options for finding a contact. This could be either by e-mail address or by searching for them from your address book. As you will probably have e-mail addresses for friends or colleagues you wish to contact, check the box for finding by e-mail address. Click the **Next** button.

6   Enter the e-mail address of the person you wish to contact. Click the **Next** button. Click the **Finish** button in the next screen, which advises that your contact has been successfully added.

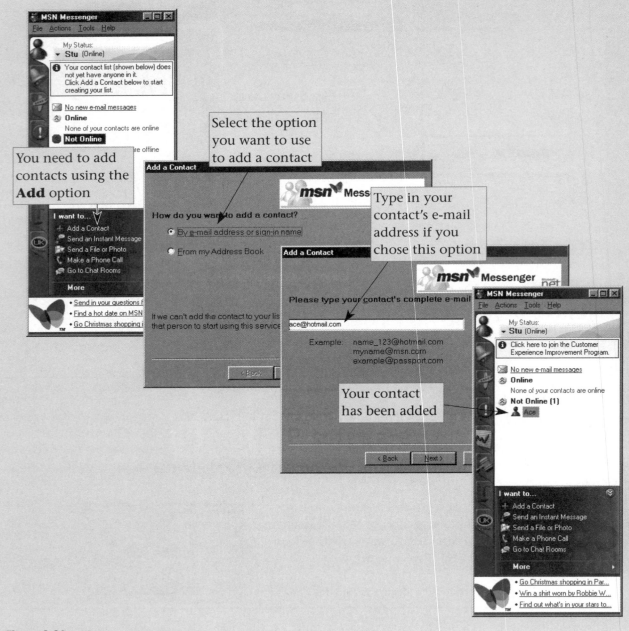

Figure 2.36 Adding a contact

Information

There are two icons on your Messenger window. One is for contacts who are online, the other for contacts who are not online. If a contact you have added to your list has also got MSN Messenger on their computer and has signed in, their name will appear next to the **Online** icon. If so, you can start exchanging messages. If not, they will be shown under the **Not Online** icon and remain there until they have signed in (assuming they too have MSN Messenger on their computer).

7 If your contact is not online you have the option to send them an e-mail.

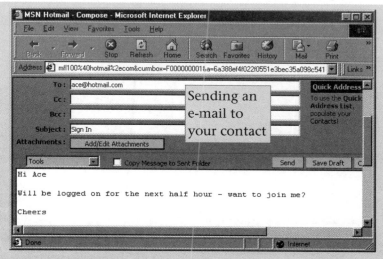

Figure 2.37 Sending e-mail to contact

8 If your contact accepts your invitation and goes online, you will see an alert to let you know. Your contact will then be shown as online in the Messenger window.

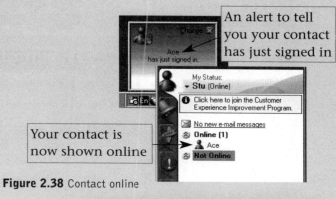

Figure 2.38 Contact online

9 If your contact is shown as being online, double click on their name and the chat window will be launched.

Enter your message and click on **Send** or press the **Enter** key

Figure 2.39 Enter message

10 Enter your message in the lower message pane and either press the **Enter** key or click the **Send** button, to dispatch your message to your contact. As they reply, their message will be shown under a copy of your message in the upper message pane. With each message sent or received, it will be added to the upper message window so that you can see the 'conversation' as it progresses.

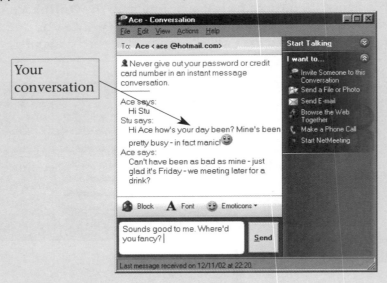

Figure 2.40 Having a conversation

11 To end the chat, select the **Close** option. You can start to chat again by double clicking on the Messenger icon in the system tray near the clock and signing in.

12 To end your session, select the **File/Sign out** option from the Messenger toolbar and then select **Close** from the same menu.

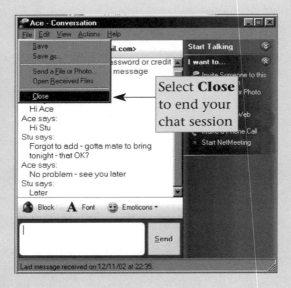

Figure 2.41 Closing chat session

You can also send files using Messenger, as well as having a voice conversation. If you want to have a voice conversation you will need speakers and a microphone (as will your online contact).

Method

I   Click on the **Send a File or Photo** option.

2   Browse your hard drive to find the file you wish to send in the **Send a File to** dialogue box and select. Click on **Open**.

3   You will be informed that Messenger is waiting for your contact to accept (or decline) the file. If your contact accepts, your file will be transferred.

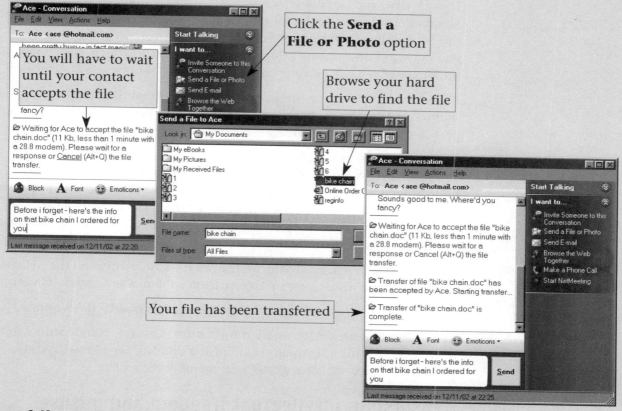

Figure 2.42 Sending files

→ Practise your skills 5

1   Connect to the Internet.

2   Select a chat room to join. Your ISP may have a chat site, or you could use one of the web-based chat sites at www.msn.co.uk, or www.freeserve.com/chat, or www.yahoo.co.uk/chat. You might find that joining one of the chat rooms on a site such as the BBC web site at www.bbc.co.uk would be interesting.

3   Locate the Help information and print out a copy of the details for future reference. It may be an FAQ page or some similar help feature.

4   Join in a chat room which interests you. A chat room for newcomers may well be a good idea until you get used to chatting.

5   Log out of the service when you decide to leave the chat room.

6   Exit your browser and disconnect from the Internet.

The relevance and implications of the Internet

The Internet is an exciting place to discover, but such a powerful medium has made many changes to the way we communicate and do our daily work, which must have both benefits and disadvantages.

Immediate access to information

Using e-mail you can communicate with other people halfway across the world almost instantly (and it may be cheaper), so the flow of information can be very quick. But just as you can communicate with others speedily, so you may find unwelcome information being sent to you, such as masses of junk mail which can be time-consuming to deal with and a nuisance.

Communication via the Internet is often less formal than conventional methods, although the more casual approach to business may mean that people could forget that an agreement by e-mail is legally binding.

Copies of documents, pictures, music clips, etc. can be sent to another computer anywhere in the world, so businesses can operate across many boundaries quickly and efficiently without the need to travel and incur large mail costs. Up-to-date information, news, weather, etc. is available at the touch of a button. You can review new software before buying it and download files, updates and bug fixes to make your computer work more effectively.

You can research practically any topic from the vast archives on the Net, and seek advice on a whole range of things, from an illness to a computer virus.

It can help people with disabilities to keep in touch with the world.

In a technological society where information is power, people who don't have access to this information can be at a disadvantage in work and education. These are often the poorer members of society.

Censorship, intellectual freedom and misuse

No one controls the Internet, which certainly allows users a great deal of freedom of speech and access, however this lack of control means it is open to misuse and exploitation. There have been attempts by governments to restrict information to their citizens, but in such a deregulated world as the Net, it isn't easy. Legislation has been passed by governments forcing ISPs to record traffic on their servers or to allow intelligence agencies to access subscribers' e-mails. Just as any organisation can set up a web site, so someone else can block it and replace it with their own information or propaganda. Finding the right balance is a very difficult task.

The Net allows just about anybody to air their views and opinions through the many networks available, such as discussion groups and web sites. This allows great freedom of speech, and organisations, such as Amnesty International, who use the Net to keep people across the world informed about abuses of human rights wherever they might occur, can use this as a vehicle to argue for change or ask for support. This could have a beneficial effect on the policy of governments. Highlighting problems in this way could bring pressure on governments from other organisations and officials to make policy changes.

The other side of this, however, is the potential misuse by organisations intent on disrupting the established order for their own causes.

There is also a great deal of concern about some of the unsuitable material on the Internet, such as pornographic material. This is especially worrying when children have access to the Internet, and online services have introduced controls over site access to try to avoid children being exposed to any unpleasant material. Tracking any abuse of such material over the Net isn't always an easy matter as many of those participating in such traffic will have found ways of hiding their tracks.

International trade and e-commerce

The world of international trade has changed over the years with the increasing use of the Internet as a means of communicating and getting business done. You no longer need to have an office on the site of the manufacture of goods. Provided there are good electronic links between sites, businesses can be run from just about anywhere in the world. This has, along with other factors, led to the globalisation of trade with an increasingly large proportion of the goods we use being produced by a small number of global corporations or companies. While this may mean that goods are produced at the most competitive prices, it can also mean that manufacture can move from country to country seeking the best conditions for production. This can have a devastating effect on employment in an area when companies close their manufacturing sites.

Increasing globalisation also means more competition, with prices of goods responding very quickly to changes in the cost of raw materials, for example, or fluctuations of the stock markets. As the information about such important factors in international trade are so speedily and effectively communicated through the electronic communication networks, companies can react very quickly.

On a more local level, e-commerce brings the world of business to the home desktop. Shopping online suits many people's busy modern lifestyles. You can buy just about anything on the Net, and it isn't restricted to your region, but can be purchased from other countries. This may mean you can get the most competitive price for the goods you want, however there are also issues about the return of goods, delivery charges and import taxes, not to mention the distance if you find the goods aren't functioning properly.

There are always security issues when using the Net, most especially if you are buying goods, and you would be well advised to deal with well-known and reliable firms. There have been recent cases involving the misuse of personal details, including bank accounts, so good security protection is of the utmost importance (this topic is covered in more detail in Section 5).

However, the Internet is a very useful facility if you live in the country far from shopping centres as you will be able to access goods and services not available locally.

As the Internet isn't controlled, it is very easy for unscrupulous people to set up sites to sell goods, which will never be sent, or services, which will never be delivered. Some companies have set up e-commerce sites in good faith and then been unable to meet all their orders and have collapsed, leaving unfulfilled orders and buyers without the goods for which they may have paid.

Access to the communication networks and equipment are essential to carry out business via the Internet. Developing countries however may not have the money to invest in technology, and so could be disadvantaged by not having access to all the information and services available. This, in the Information Age, is a disadvantage that could lead to the development of an underclass, who may never be in a position to compete with the large global empires.

Learning

There is a wealth of learning materials available on the Net. Many educational organisations, government bodies involved in education, educational institutions and individuals have uploaded information, advice, exemplars, worksheets and activities, support materials and many other learning resources which are available to anyone connected to the Net.

These resources span the whole range of age and interest, from primary education to postgraduate research. Any search on the Web will usually turn up many tens or hundreds of related pages. One of the best known educational resource banks can be found on the BBC web site (www.bbc.co.uk), where topics range from basic IT to cracking the DNA code. Much of the material available is free to use for educational purposes, which makes it a useful resource for teaching staff.

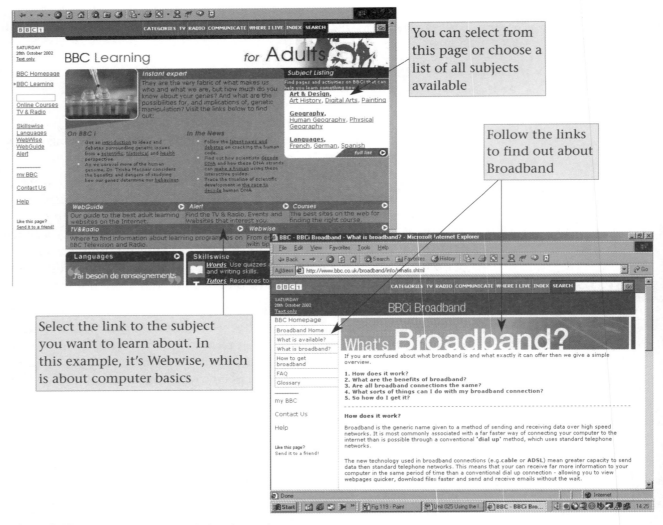

You can select from this page or choose a list of all subjects available

Follow the links to find out about Broadband

Select the link to the subject you want to learn about. In this example, it's Webwise, which is about computer basics

Figure 2.43 The Internet is a valuable learning tool

Many educational and business organisations are using **Virtual Learning Environments (VLE)** to support students' learning. Access to course documents, tests, assignments and even e-mail and live chat can be available through this medium. Students can study from the comfort of their own home and access the materials they may need (or may have missed through non-attendance!) via their Internet connection. One such VLE, used in an FE college, is shown in the following screen shots.

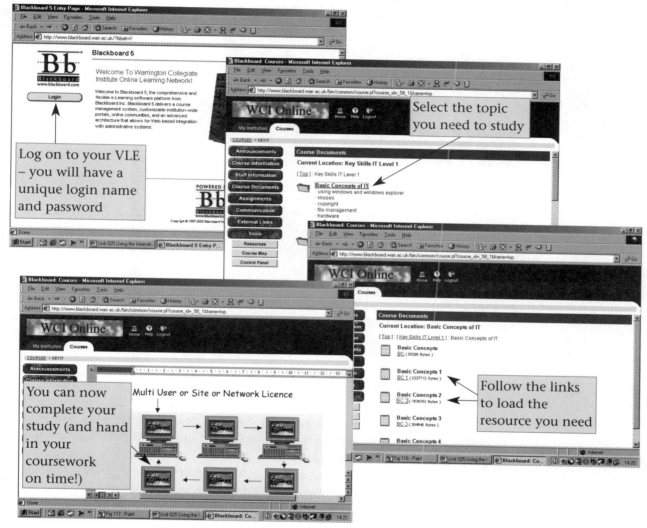

Figure 2.44 An example of a VLE

Learndirect is an online learning service which aims to help people learn and update their skills using a wide range of interactive and multimedia resource material. You can take a whole course, or just a unit or two, it depends on what you need. You can study from home or enrol on a Learndirect course at your local college, library, or many other places.

Figure 2.45 The Learndirect site

Viruses

There is always the threat of a maliciously developed virus being transferred across the Internet whenever you are connected. These can be transmitted via e-mail attachments or downloaded files, or put on your computer by hackers and intruders to your system. Viruses can vary from the fairly innocuous ones which just flash up a message or bleep now and again, to the devastating ones which can trash your hard drive completely. At best they are a nuisance, at worst they can mean great expense and loss of valuable data and information.

It is essential to have an up-to-date virus utility installed on your computer and used regularly. Many commercial products can be set to check your system at regular intervals to see if a virus has been able to penetrate your defences and to ensure that it is made harmless. Some products can scan all your e-mails and any files you download to stop a virus before it gets onto your system. As traffic over the Net increases, so does the risk of a virus finding its way onto your computer. This is especially true of 'always on' connections, such as Broadband, where intruders will have plenty of opportunity to test your computer's defences! (There is more about Internet security in Section 5.)

Copyright/licensing

There is legislation in most countries against using other people's material without permission, however it isn't always easy to ensure that copyright or licence requirements are met. Many of the shadowy sites on the margins of the Internet will pedal pirated software and organisations such as FAST (Federation Against Software Theft) have been unable to eradicate such practices. Files can be transferred at the flick of a switch and tracking all the billions of data movements over the Net can be a massive task. One of the biggest recent cases of infringement of copyright led to the closure of a web site involved in the illegal distribution of music over the Net. It is therefore very important to read the small print on web pages or software sites before downloading files and using them for your own purposes. (There is more about copyright and licensing in Section 5.)

→ **Practise your skills 6**

1　Using your FTP software, locate a site which provides access to etexts.

2　Locate a suitable ebook, and download to your computer.

3　Use your browser to locate the same site and repeat the process for another etext.

4　Open a new word processing document and write brief notes about the two processes and indicate which one you prefer, giving your reasons.

5　Print out your document.

→ **Practise your skills 7**

1　Sign into your favourite chat site and identify suitable discussion groups on a hobby you enjoy.

2　Participate in a chat session on your chosen hobby.

3　Log on to your news server and identify newsgroups on the same hobby you selected in the chat session.

4　Subscribe to the newsgroup and select several messages to see what the current postings are about.

5　Make brief notes about the two ways of exchanging information about your hobby and identify the advantages and disadvantages of each.

→ **Practise your skills 8**

1　Set up an instant messaging program on your computer and ask a friend (it may be a good idea to team up with someone else working through this section!) to do the same (remember, you will need the same instant messaging program on both computers).

2　Add your friend's e-mail address to your contact list and take a screen print of the messaging window. Print out a copy.

3　Log on to your messaging service and check to see if your contact (friend) is online and ready to talk.

4　Exchange messages about your hobby with your contact.

5　Log off your messaging service.

→ Check your knowledge 3

1 What should you always do before opening a file downloaded from the Internet?

2 If you were downloading a program from the Internet, which option would you select in the **File Download** dialogue box?

3 What would you probably have to do after you've downloaded a program to your hard drive?

4 How does an FTP site address differ from a web address?

5 What is the main difference between a newsgroup and chat?

6 Why would you not enter a message to a newsgroup in capital letters?

7 What is the main difference between web-based chat and Internet chat?

8 What do the initials IRC stand for?

9 Who or what controls the Internet?

10 In your opinion, what is the most serious implication of the growth in the use of the Internet?

Consolidation 1

1 Using appropriate search techniques, search for ten learning resources or information on dinosaurs.

2 Create a folder in your Favorites to store the URLs of useful sites you identify. Add sites to this folder as you do your research.

3 Produce a screen print of your folder when you have added all the sites and print out a copy.

4 Reload the three sites which contained the material you found most interesting.

5 Download copies of the three resources you found to your computer and save in a new folder, appropriately named, on your hard drive.

6 Log on to the message board at the BBC web site and select the group where the discussion topic is dinosaurs.

7 Identify a discussion title which relates to your own research and post a reply asking for more information or recommendations for other sites of interest. (You will need to register at the site before you can post a reply.)

8 Using an instant messaging program, contact a friend (preferably one who is doing this same activity) and exchange the web addresses of the sites you have found. Take a screen print of the conversation and produce a printout.

9 Check the discussion group where you posted your message to see if there are any replies (you may have to wait a day or two before you get a reply).

10 Note down any web sites recommended, and enter each URL in your browser Address bar in turn to access the contents.

11 Download any further useful information from these sites to the folder you created in step 5.

12 Using My Computer or Windows Explorer, browse your hard drive to locate the folder with your saved resources. Take a screen print of the contents and print out a copy.

13 Start a new word processing document and write a report on your experience of completing this activity. What implications for study and learning can you draw from it?

Note: It is assumed that you will connect and disconnect to the Internet as required throughout this exercise. Ensure that you close all programs after use.

You will learn to

- Identify advantages and disadvantages of using web-based e-mail
- Create and use a web-based e-mail account
- Use automated methods to reply to e-mail messages
  - □ Identify potential problems of using automated reply methods
- Maintain an address book
  - □ Add addresses
  - □ Delete addresses
  - □ Edit existing addresses
  - □ Set up and maintain groups
- Create and send messages to e-mail groups
- Identify the advantages of using an address book

Introduction: E-mail

One of the quickest ways of communicating with others on a network is to use **electronic mail**, or **e-mail** as it is usually called. You can use the e-mail program provided by your ISP, usually included with your browser (this is usually either Outlook Express or Netscape Navigator), or a web-based e-mail account or perhaps both.

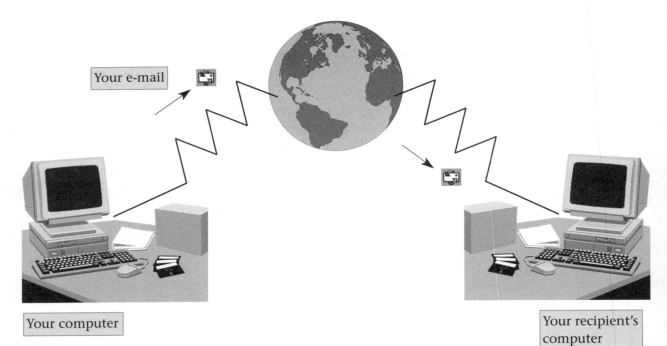

Your e-mail

Your computer

Your recipient's computer

Figure 3.1 Sending e-mail

Web-based e-mail

With Outlook Express and other e-mail programs loaded onto your computer, you can compose your e-mails when you are offline and just connect to the Net to send (and check) your mail. This saves considerable money in call charges but can be a problem if you need to check your mail when you are away from home. You can certainly connect to your ISP wherever you may be, but can you imagine the call cost if you were sunning yourself on a tropical beach? This is when web-based e-mail can be a good option. Instead of using a dedicated e-mail program, you can create a free account with a web-based e-mail service such as Hotmail or Excite mail.

Information

Many ISPs are now providing the facility to access your mail, which is on their mail server, from anywhere in the world, or you may be able to arrange to have your ordinary mail forwarded to a Hotmail or other web-based e-mail account. Your ISP will have further details.

You will have a new e-mail address which will be similar to josie@hotmail.com. Being web-based, you can read and write your e-mails by logging on to your e-mail service and entering your personal username and password. It doesn't then matter where you are in the world, you can still pick up your mail and reply using any of the cyber cafés or hotel Internet facilities which are available in many places across the globe. It can be very useful to have both an e-mail facility provided by your ISP and a web-based e-mail address, but you will have to make sure that people know which one to use and when to use it if you are going away.

There are some disadvantages to using web-based e-mail, however:

- You still need a way of connecting to the Internet, probably provided by an ISP.
- You have to be online to read and write your e-mails, which could soon begin to mount up to quite a cost in call charges.
- You can only read your e-mails while you are online. Once you disconnect from the Internet you can't then quickly check a message's contents when you've forgotten some detail without re-connecting, as your e-mails stay on the provider's server.
- Many web-based e-mail accounts will only have a certain amount of space allocated for mail. In the case of a free Hotmail account, this is 2 MB, and if messages mount up to more than the 2 MB allowed, some messages will be removed. Once they have been removed, they cannot be recovered. As 2 MB isn't a great deal of space, your messages can soon reach this limit, especially if you are sent messages with attachments. Maintaining your account through good housekeeping will be very important.
- There is often a time limit set on how infrequently you can use your e-mail account. In a free Hotmail account for example, if you don't access your account for 30 days it will be marked 'inactive' and all e-mails, addresses and folders will be deleted.
- Some web-based e-mail accounts seem more prone to spam and junk mail than others, although most will have fairly advanced filtering facilities.

Create and use web-based e-mail

Task 3.1   Creating a web-based e-mail account (using Hotmail for this example)

Method

1. Connect to the Internet.
2. Load the web page for Hotmail at www.hotmail.com.
3. Complete the form with your details.
4. **Sign in**.

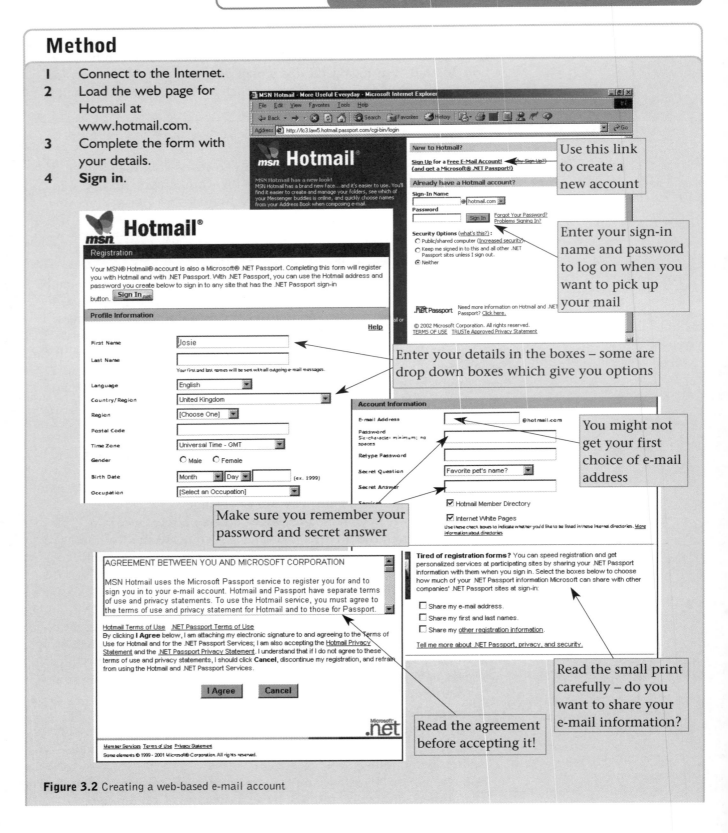

Figure 3.2 Creating a web-based e-mail account

Now you can collect your e-mail wherever you are.

Information

The screen shots which follow use Hotmail as the web-based e-mail account, although the procedures will be very similar for most other web-based accounts.

| Task 3.2 | Receiving messages with a web-based e-mail account |

Method

1   Log on to your web-based e-mail server.
2   Enter your username and password and sign in.
3   Click on your **Inbox** folder.

Information

Your Inbox details will tell you if you have new mail.

You could use the Inbox tab along the top of the mail window to access your messages.

4   Click on the message you want to read.

Information

You will be able to see an envelope icon by the side of the message to show that you have a new message

5   Read your message in the message pane and choose your next action. You may want to save it, reply to it, print it or even forward it to someone else.

Information

You can see the details about the message in the header, for example who sent the message, when it was sent and if, as in the example shown, there is an attachment.

6   Access the attachment by clicking the attachment details in the message header to open the attachment window.

Information

You should always be aware that viruses can be transmitted by e-mail attachments. In Hotmail, all attachments are automatically scanned by McAfee virus software.

7 Click on the **Download File** button.

8 Select the option you want from the **File Download** dialogue box.

Information

You can choose to save the file to disk, which would be useful if you wanted to view the file later offline, or open the file from the current location, which will allow you to view the file whilst online.

9 Sign out from your account to close it.

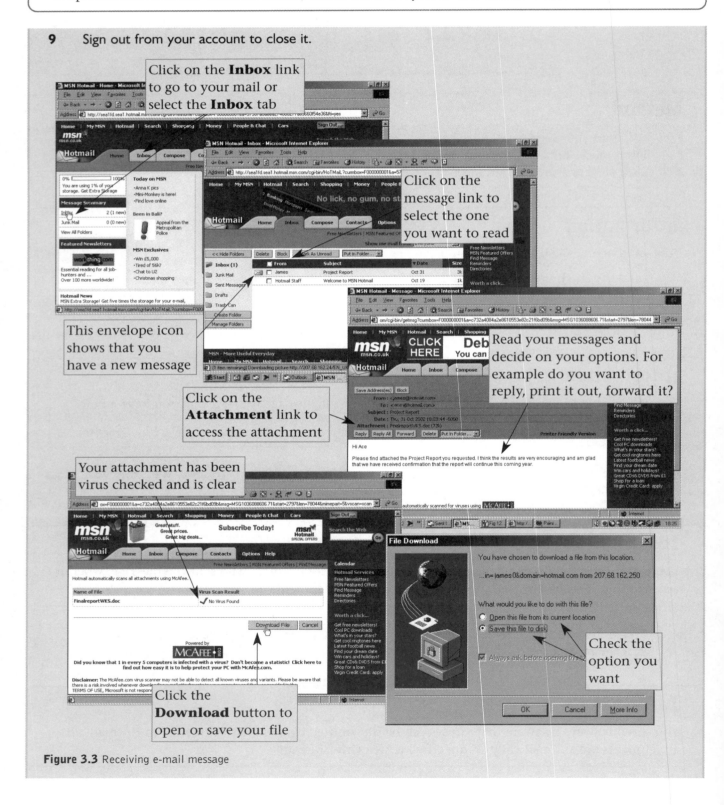

Figure 3.3 Receiving e-mail message

Task 3.3 Sending a message using a web-based e-mail account

Method

1. Log on to your web-based e-mail server.
2. Enter your username and password and sign in.
3. Select the **Compose** tab.
4. Enter the e-mail address of your recipient or, if the address has been added to the **Quick Address List**, select it from the list shown.

Information

Your **Quick Address List** in Hotmail will only show five addresses. To access other addresses you can click the **Show All** button, or use the **Contact** tab.

5. Enter a suitable title in the **Subject** box.
6. Enter your text in the message box.
7. Attach any files you wish to send using the **Add/Edit Attachments** button.
8. Send your message by clicking on the **Send** button.

Information

You can save the sent message by checking the **Copy Message to Sent Folder** box.

9. Sign out from your account to close it.

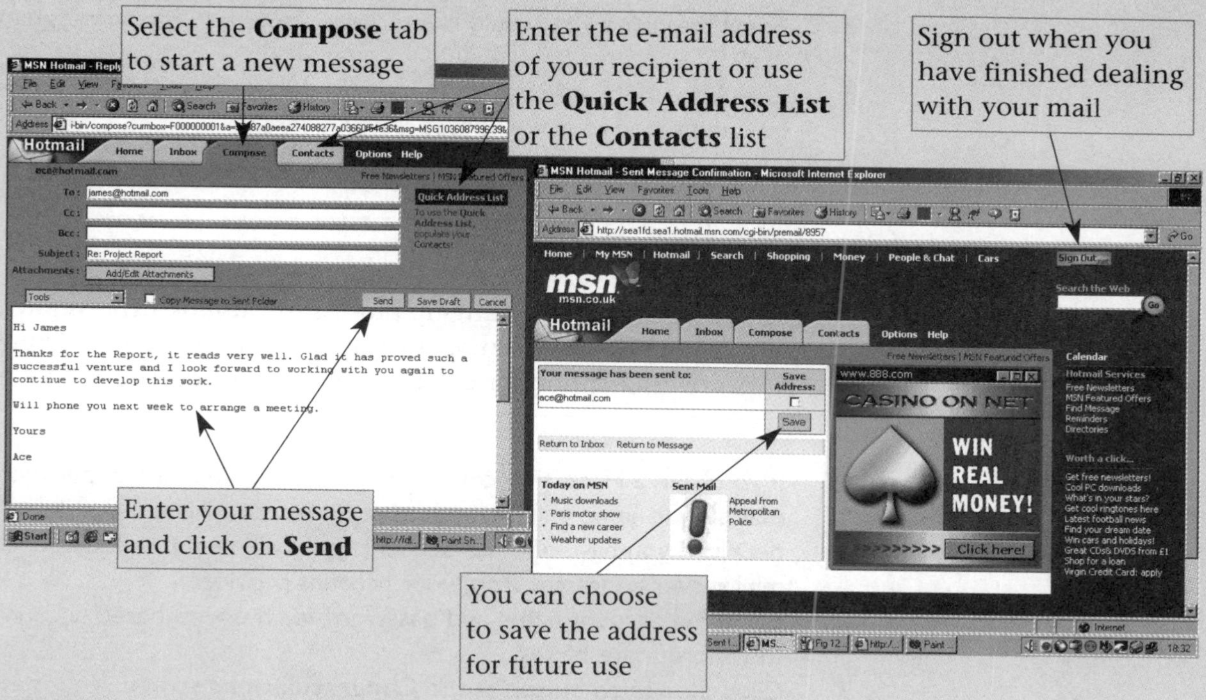

Figure 3.4 Sending an e-mail message

Having both a web-based e-mail account and one provided by your ISP can give you the flexibility to send and receive e-mails from home and away. If you have a web-based e-mail account it may be useful to set up Outlook Express to check your web-based account at the same time as it checks your ISP account.

Information

The screen shots which follow use Hotmail as the web-based e-mail account. You will need your web-based account provider's mail server addresses for other e-mail accounts.

Method

1   With Outlook Express open, select **Accounts** from the **Tools** menu.
2   In the **Internet Accounts** dialogue box click on the **Add** button and select **Mail** from the pop-up menu which appears.

Information

Click on the **Next** button after completing each instruction to move to the next screen.

3   Enter the name you would like to have displayed on your outgoing e-mails.
4   Check the **I already have an e-mail address that I'd like to use** box and enter your web-based e-mail address.

Information

This screen is part of the setting-up process in Outlook Express 5 where you can also opt to set up a new Hotmail account. In Outlook Express 6 there is only the option for entering your e-mail address.

5   If you have a Hotmail account, the information needed about the e-mail server name will be entered automatically. Accept the default details. If you have another account, you will need the details of the mail server addresses from your account provider.
6   Enter the account name and password for the web-based account in the appropriate boxes.
7   Click the **Finish** button at the **Congratulations** screen. Your new account will be shown in the **Internet Accounts** listings.

Information

You can choose your default e-mail account by selecting the account name in the list and clicking the **Set as Default** button.

When you log on to your ISP's server to collect your mail, Outlook Express will automatically check your web-based account for new mail too.

Information

You can follow the same process to include other ISP e-mail accounts in Outlook Express, but you will need their mail server addresses.

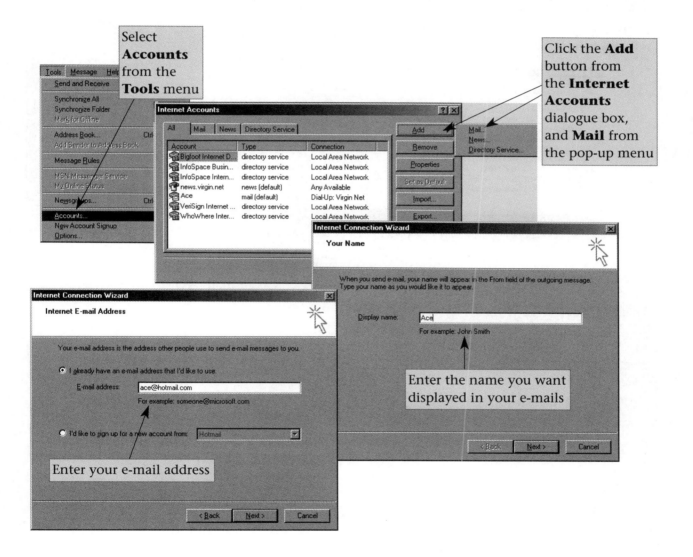

Select **Accounts** from the **Tools** menu

Click the **Add** button from the **Internet Accounts** dialogue box, and **Mail** from the pop-up menu

Enter your e-mail address

Enter the name you want displayed in your e-mails

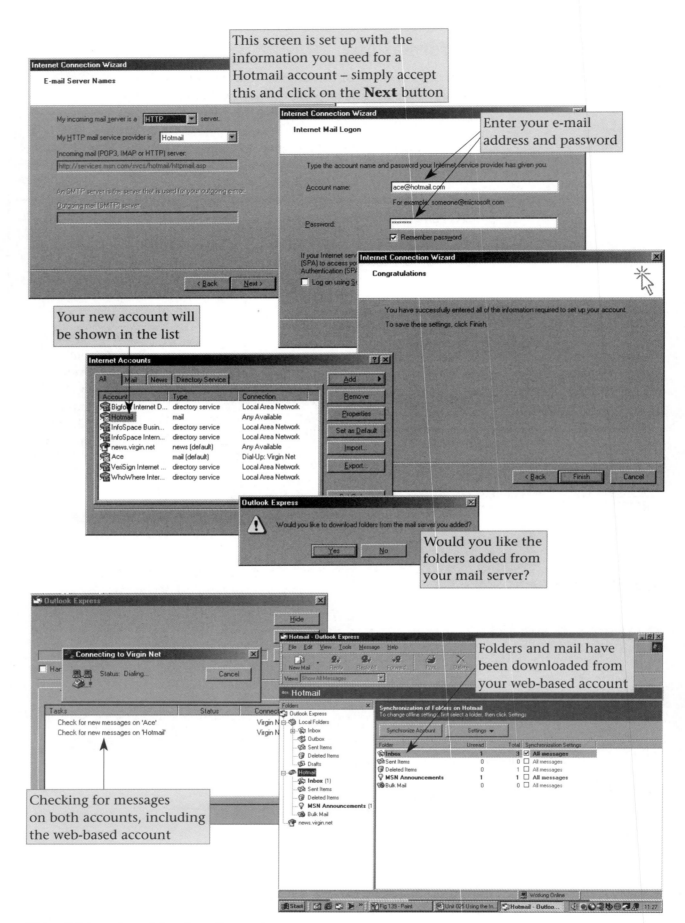

Figure 3.5 Accessing web-based e-mail account

Information

Although you can access your web-based e-mail account through Outlook Express, you will need to be online to read any messages. You can make sure that messages are available offline by synchronising folders. From the **Folders** list, select a mail server. Then select the **All messages** or **New messages only** checkbox for the items you want to read offline and choose **Synchronize All** from the **Tools** menu.

→ Practise your skills 1

1 Set up a web-based e-mail account.
2 Using your ISP e-mail account, send an e-mail message to your new web-based account.
3 Access your web-based account and read your message.
4 Print out a copy of the message.
5 Compose and send a reply.
6 Access your ISP account and check for new mail.
7 Print off a copy of the message you have received.

Automated reply methods

Task 3.5   Using automated reply methods

If you are away from your computer and wish to let the people who have sent e-mails know, you can set up an automated reply to say you are not available.

Method

1 Start a new mail message and enter the text you want to send back to those who e-mail you.
2 Save the file to your hard drive using the **Save As** function in the **File** menu.
3 Select the **Mail** option from the **Message Rules** option in the **Tools** menu.
4 In Section 1 of the **New Mail Rule** dialogue box, select the first condition for your rule. In this example it is the **Where the From line contains people** option.
5 In Section 3, select the underlined link **contains people**.
6 Enter the e-mail addresses of the people you want to include in the message rule and click **Add** after entering each address. When all addresses have been added, click on **OK**.
7 In Section 2, select the second condition for your rule. In this example it is the **Reply with message** option.
8 In Section 3, select the underlined link **message**.
9 Select the saved message file from the appropriate place on your hard drive.
10 Both your conditions will now be shown in the **New Message Rules** Section 3.
11 Click in the box in Section 4, and enter a name for your rule – in this case it is **Holiday**.
12 Click on **OK** and the **Message Rule** dialogue box shows that your rule is now operational. Click on **OK** to accept.

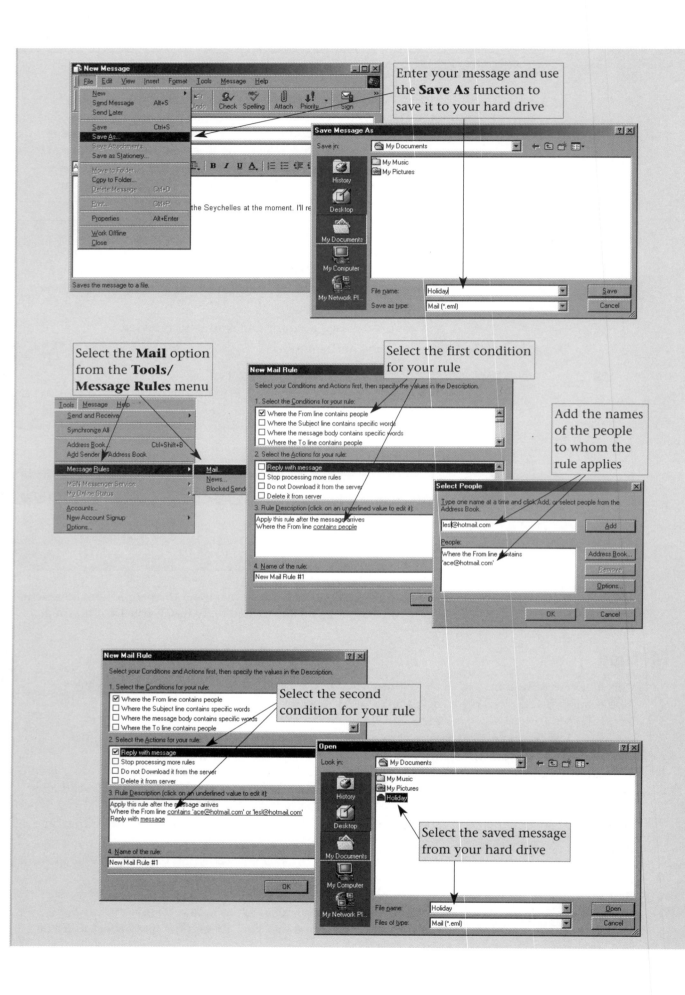

Enter your message and use the **Save As** function to save it to your hard drive

Select the **Mail** option from the **Tools/Message Rules** menu

Select the first condition for your rule

Add the names of the people to whom the rule applies

Select the second condition for your rule

Select the saved message from your hard drive

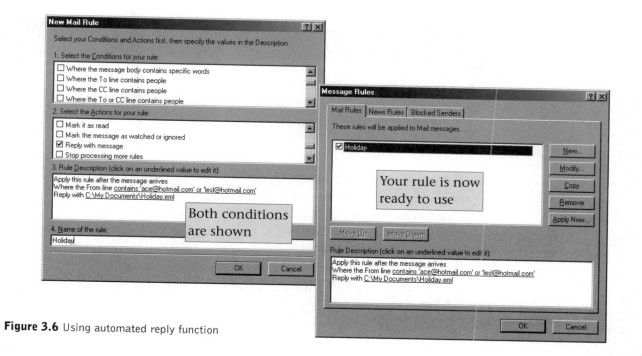

Figure 3.6 Using automated reply function

Information

You will need to be online to use this automated reply function. This would mean either leaving your computer switched on and connected to your ISP permanently, or setting it up to dial up your ISP at regular intervals. Both these options would mean your computer would have to be switched on all the time you were away. This might cause you some concern as many people wouldn't like to leave their machines on for such a period of time. The other consideration is the potential costs of either option, especially leaving your machine connected to your ISP for the whole period you were away. If you pay phone bills which vary with the amount of time spent online, it could get very expensive indeed, especially at peak rates.

If your recipients have also set up automated reply functions, you could find yourself in a loop, with messages being sent backwards and forwards!

Sometimes, even with the best intentions, getting an automated reply when you need an urgent answer can be very annoying.

If you are in a conference and messages are sent, it could cause problems with an automated reply being sent back.

→ Practise your skills 2

1 Set up an automated reply in your ISP e-mail account to respond to a message from your web-based e-mail account.

2 Log on to your web-based e-mail account and send a message to your ISP account.

3 Check your web-based e-mail account after a suitable period to see if your automated reply has been received.

4 Print out a copy of the message.

Address book

Just as your paper-based address book holds information about family, friends and other contacts, so your e-mail program offers a similar electronic facility. The main difference is that you don't need to write the details by hand, or have lots of crossings out as addresses change over time – it's much easier with your electronic version!

Most address book facilities in e-mail programs allow you to enter more details than just the bare name and e-mail address. You will find that you can also enter other useful information, including home addresses and phone numbers, business details, and even important dates such as birthdays and anniversaries.

Task 3.6 Accessing the address book

Method

1   Open your e-mail program.
2   Click on the **Addresses** button on the toolbar [Addresses], or select the **Address Book** from the **Tools** menu.
3   The **Address Book** will open.

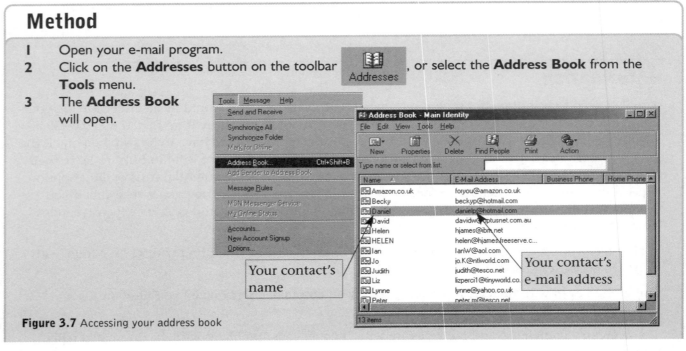

Figure 3.7 Accessing your address book

Address Book toolbar

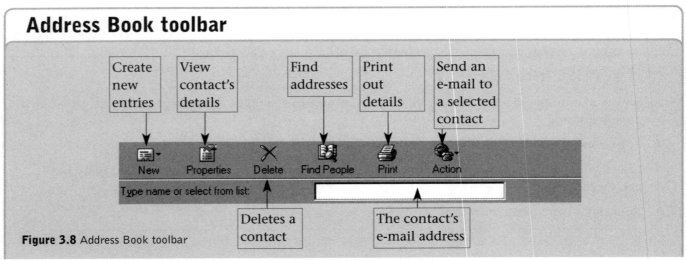

Figure 3.8 Address Book toolbar

- **New** This option allows you to create a new entry in your address book.
- **Properties** You can view the details of each contact in your address book.
- **Delete** When you no longer want to keep an address in your address book you can use this option to delete the details.
- **Find People** Use this option to search for specific people in your address book. This can be very useful if you find that you've got a large number of addresses and scrolling through them all gets time-consuming.
- **Print** This option allows you to print information about the selected contact or contacts.
- **Action** Amongst other options, you can choose to send mail to the selected contact.

Task 3.7 | Adding addresses

Method 1 From an open message

1 Right click the mouse on the message in the message list and select **Add Sender to Address Book** from the pop-up menu.
2 The address is added automatically to your address book.

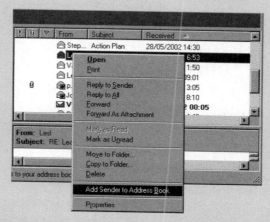

Figure 3.9 One way of adding addresses automatically

Or

1 With the message selected, choose **Add to Sender Address Book** from the **Tools** menu.
2 The address is added automatically to your address book.

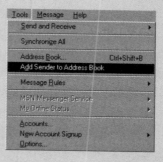

Figure 3.10 Another way of adding addresses automatically

Method 2 Entering an address manually

1   Open the address book.
2   Select **New Contact** from the **File** menu or the drop down menu from the **New** button on the toolbar.
3   In the **Properties** box, enter the details of your new contact, including their name, nickname and e-mail address in the boxes under the **Name** tab.
4   Click on the **Add** button to add the e-mail address to your address book.
5   Enter any other details you want to record under the other tabs available, such as birthday, business address, etc.
6   Click on **OK** to close the Properties box.

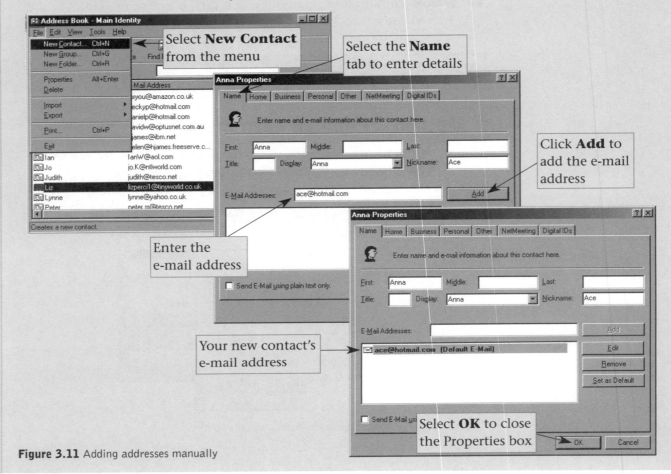

Figure 3.11 Adding addresses manually

Information

Instead of the whole e-mail address or the name appearing in the **contact** list, you can give your contact an e-mail nickname and select this to be displayed. Enter the nickname in the appropriate field in the contact's Properties box, and select the name you want to use from the drop down list box in the **Display** field.

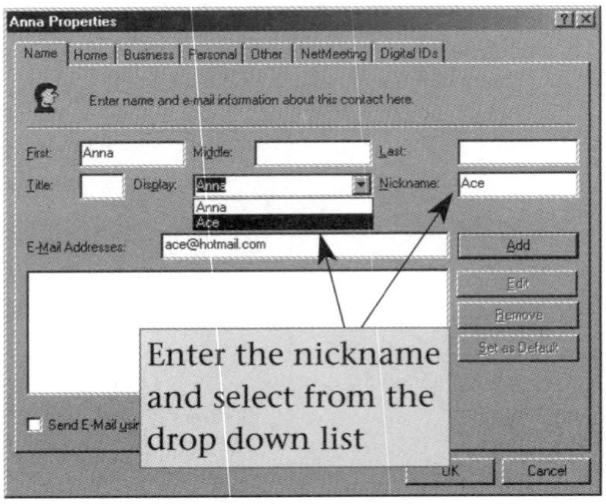

Figure 3.12 Entering a nickname

You may find over time that some of the contact details may no longer be valid. Perhaps they may have new e-mail addresses, or perhaps you no longer send messages to them. Whatever the reason, you will have addresses that you no longer want, and then you can delete them to make your address book less cluttered.

Method

1	Open the address book.
2	Select the contact you want to delete.
3	Select **Delete** from the **File** menu, or press the **Delete** key on your keyboard.
4	Click on **OK** in the warning box which appears (just as long as you are sure you want to delete the contact details).
5	Check that the contact details have been deleted from the address book and close it.

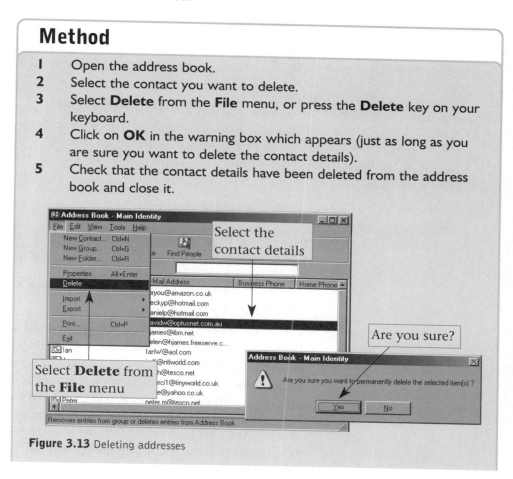

Figure 3.13 Deleting addresses

Task 3.9   Editing addresses

Sometimes you may need to change or edit an address in your address book; for example if you had the address slightly wrong correcting it would be easier than re-entering it all again.

Method

1	Open the address book.
2	Select the contact you want to edit.
3	Select **Properties** from the **File** menu, or click the **Properties** button ⬚ Properties on the toolbar.
4	Select the **Name** tab, and click the **Edit** button.
5	Edit the address.
6	Click on **OK** to implement the change.

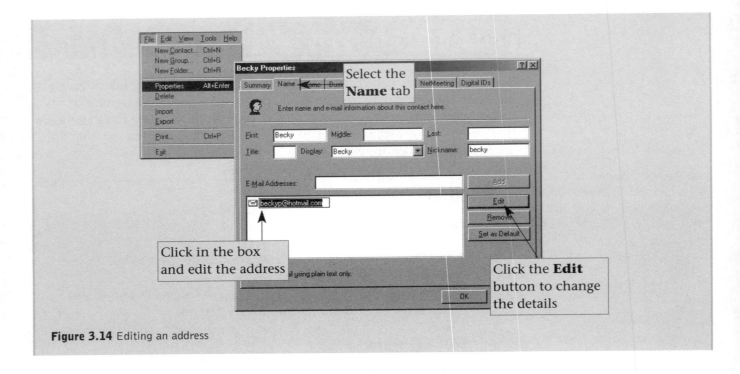

Figure 3.14 Editing an address

Aliases

The word **alias** can be used in two different contexts when sending and receiving e-mails.

Many ISPs offer a number of different e-mail addresses which all come through a shared e-mail account and are referred to as **aliases**. This would be useful if several members of a family used the same e-mail account, as each member could have their own e-mail address, or alias. For example, if you have a Freeserve account you could have e-mail addresses such as Joe@cheznous.freeserve.co.uk, Sarah@cheznous.freeserve.co.uk, and Work@cheznous.freeserve.co.uk, which will all use the same mailbox facility. To sort the incoming messages you would need to set up folders for each address and use the Message Rules options to make sure that everyone's e-mails ended up in their own Inbox.

An **alias** is also used as the name of a group of contacts in an address book. If you find that you often send the same e-mail to a group of people, you can create a single group to use instead. You can then select the group name or alias from the contact list, which is much quicker than having to use all the individual addresses. It may also mean that you don't leave someone out of the correspondence by accident – it might cause offence if you did!

Task 3.10 — Creating contact groups or aliases

Method

1 Open the address book.
2 Select **New Group** from the drop down menu of the **New** button, or from the **File** menu.

3   In the **Group Properties** box enter the Group Name.
4   Click on the **Select Members** button to open the list of contacts in the address book.
5   Select each contact you want to add to your group and click the **Select** button to add the details to the right-hand pane.
6   Click on **OK** to enter the names in your group in the Group Properties box.
7   Click on **OK** to return to your address book. The new group is shown in the list of contacts in bold type.

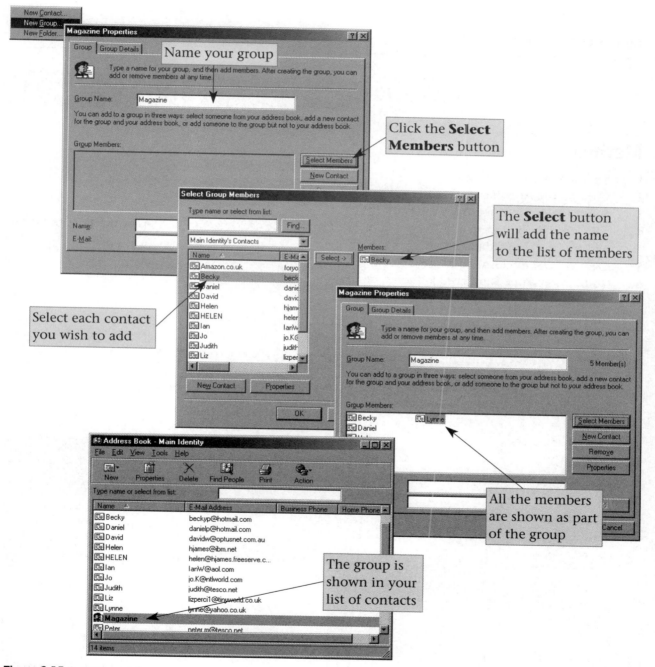

Figure 3.15 Creating an alias

Information

There are several ways to organise your address book to help you find a contact or groups more easily. You can sort them alphabetically by first or last name, by e-mail address, or by phone number by clicking on the particular heading at the top of the column. You could also use the **Sort By** option in the **View** menu.

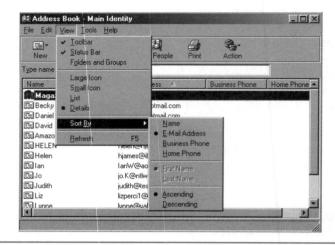

Figure 3.16 Organising your address book

Task 3.11 — Sending e-mails to your group

Method

1   Start a new mail message.
2   Click on the Address Book icon next to the **To:** box.
3   Select the group name from the contact list.
4   Click the **To:** button to add the group to the **To:** box, or click the **Cc:** button, or the **Bcc:** button to add the group to either of these fields.
5   Click on **OK** to close the address book.
6   Your group name is entered in the chosen field.
7   Complete your message and send as usual.

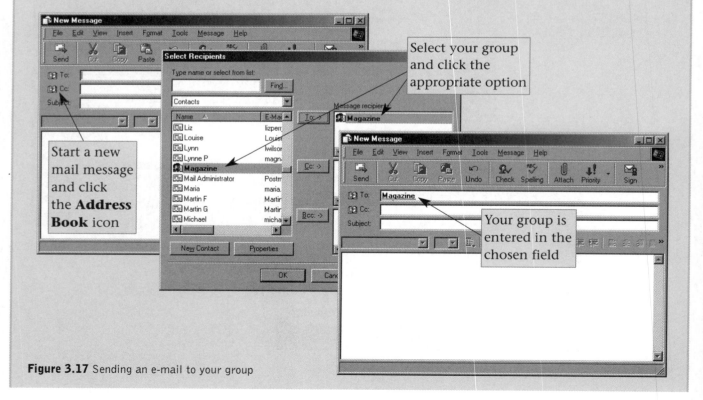

Figure 3.17 Sending an e-mail to your group

Advantages of using an address book

- Access to contact details is quick.
- You don't need to remember all the dots and domain names for your contacts, thus reducing the risk of typing in an incorrect address and having your e-mail 'bounced' (sent back undelivered).
- You can select several recipients at the same time and send copy messages to any contacts using the address book lists.
- You can edit contact details if they change.
- You can delete contacts you no longer need.
- You can have addresses entered automatically from new contacts.
- You can add addresses manually if you have new details to enter.
- You can keep details of other information such as home or business addresses as well as e-mail addresses.
- You can send information to everyone in your address book. This might be useful if you need to tell everyone about your own contact detail changes.
- You can create groups so that you can send the same message to a group of people at the same time without having to enter their details individually.
- You can sort your address book in a number of ways to suit the task you need to do.
- You can print out all or just selected contact details.
- You can search for a contact using the **Edit/Find** option.
- You can change the view to suit your needs by using the **View** menu.
- You can use your address book in other programs such as Word.

Information

There is one big disadvantage of the address book. Some of the viruses which can invade your machine can replicate themselves and then send a copy to everyone in your contacts list. You can imagine that you might not be very popular if you have a large contact list! This is a very good reason to have a virus checker which you use and update regularly.

→ Practise your skills 3

1   Open your word processing program and enter details of the advantages of using a web-based e-mail account.
2   Save the file to your hard drive with the file name **web-based account**.
3   Compose a message in your ISP e-mail account to your web-based account to say you are attaching a file about the advantages of having a web-based account.
4   Attach your file **web-based account**.
5   Send the message.
6   Log on to your web-based e-mail account and read your new messages.
7   Access the attachment and save it to your hard drive in a different location to the original file.
8   Open your word processing program and load the file you have received.
9   Print out a copy.

→ Practise your skills 4

1 Load your ISP e-mail program and open your address book.

2 Check that your web-based e-mail account is entered in the address book.

3 Take a screen print of the address book and print out a copy.

4 Enter the following addresses in your address book:

   a julian101@hotmail.com

   b c.parker@hillcollege.ac.uk

   c alison.hillyard@prda.org.uk

   d ajmackintosh@wcicoll.ac.uk

5 Create a contact group for these addresses with the name **Training**.

6 Take a screen print of your address book to show this contact group and save it to your hard drive with the filename **training**.

7 Compose a new message to your web-based e-mail account and attach the file **training**.

8 Send your e-mail.

9 Set up your ISP e-mail account to check for messages on your web-based account.

10 Log on to your ISP account and check for new messages.

11 View your attachment and print out a copy.

→ Check your knowledge 1

1 Why might having both an ISP e-mail account and a web-based account be useful?

2 List two advantages and two disadvantages of using a web-based e-mail account.

3 Why would having the facility to access your web-based e-mail account from your ISP account be useful?

4 Why might you set up an automated reply?

5 What are the potential disadvantages of using the automated reply function?

6 What details, other than a contact's e-mail address, might you enter in your address book?

7 How would you delete an address from your address book?

8 Why would you set up a contact group in your address book?

9 How could you organise your address book to have your contacts sorted alphabetically by first name?

10 What do you think are the three most important advantages to using an address book function?

Section 4 | Internet conferencing

You will learn to

- Access and use a conferencing program to:
  - ☐ make conference calls
  - ☐ receive conference calls
  - ☐ use a whiteboard facility
  - ☐ transfer files
  - ☐ exit a conference call
- Describe the basic functions of a conferencing program
  - ☐ to enable real-time communication
  - ☐ to use video, sound, writing, whiteboard

Introduction: Why use Internet conferencing?

E-mail is a great way to send and receive messages, files and programs, but it is limited if you want to exchange information in real-time. Chat programs are useful if you want to exchange information in real-time, but they don't let you transfer files. A video link would be good if you wanted to see the person on the other end of your phone line, and being able to talk (voice, not text) as well would be even better. All these facilities and more are available in a conferencing program. A whiteboard can allow everyone in the conference to see and add to plans and drawings, and documents can be shared and changed to respond to suggestions from participants.

A conference can be a private affair between two people, or include many people at different locations across the world. Its use in business can remove the necessity for people to travel to a meeting, saving considerable amounts of time and expense, as conferencing can be carried out from the home or office. This would enable you to hold a conference with someone in Australia for the cost of a local phone call.

Conferencing programs are also a valuable resource in education. Using such programs, students can access a virtual classroom and both see and hear their tutor through the link. Coursework can be discussed and shared and ideas, suggestions, questions and answers can all be exchanged between those taking part. Demonstrations using the whiteboard can help understanding and files can be transferred to give students their course notes – or perhaps, the latest assignment!

To use all the facilities of a conferencing program will require:

- A computer with a connection to the Internet.
- A sound card, speakers and a microphone.
- A video camera or web cam.
- A conferencing program such as Microsoft NetMeeting.
- A fast connection to the Internet, especially for video conferencing, otherwise the pictures could be jerky and slow.

A conferencing program

Microsoft NetMeeting

Microsoft NetMeeting is installed with the Windows operating system, and can be used to hold a conference. You can access the program through the **Start/Programs/Accessories/Communications** menus by clicking on the NetMeeting item.

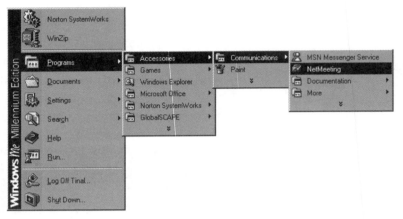

Figure 4.1 Accessing NetMeeting

Task 4.1   Configuring NetMeeting

Method

I   Load NetMeeting and enter your details in the appropriate fields in the dialogue box which appears. You must complete the name and e-mail address fields, but the others are not compulsory.

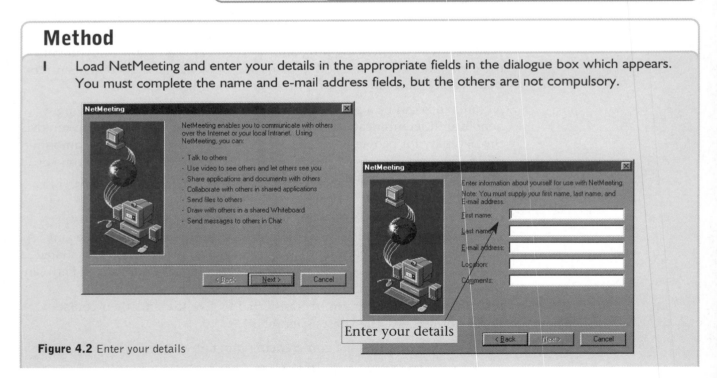

Figure 4.2 Enter your details

Information

Click on the **Next** button when you have completed each screen to move on to the next one.

2 Check the **Log on to a directory server when NetMeeting starts** box and select the directory server you want to use. This will probably be shown as Microsoft Internet Directory in the drop down list box, but if not, select it from the list.

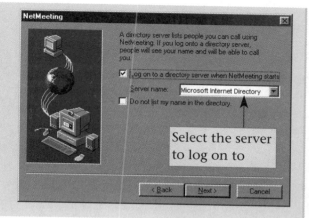

Figure 4.3 Select server

Information

If you do not want to appear in the directory listing, make sure the check box at the side of the **Do not list my name in the directory** option is ticked. This will ensure that you don't receive calls from people you don't know.

3 Select the appropriate option for how you will connect to the Internet. If you are connecting from home via your modem and phone line, this will probably be the **28000 bps or faster modem** check box.

Figure 4.4 Connection speed

4 Select whether you want a shortcut icon on your desktop and/or an icon on the Quick Launch bar.

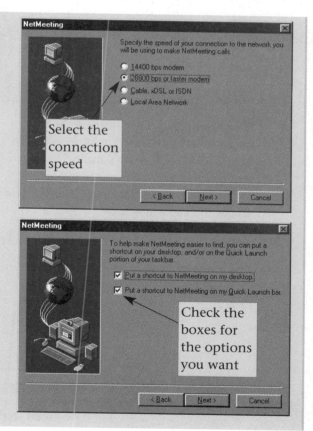

Figure 4.5 Choose shortcut

5 Read the dialogue boxes explaining about adjusting the audio settings and ensure that you check any other play and record sound programs are closed (you will need to check that your speakers are switched on though).

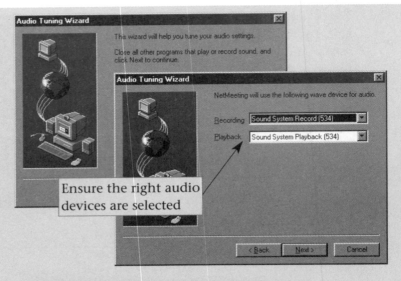

Ensure the right audio devices are selected

Figure 4.6 Choose audio settings

6 Click on the **Test** button in the **Audio Test** dialogue box which appears to hear a sample sound and adjust the volume slider to a suitable level. Click on the **Stop** button when you've finished the test.

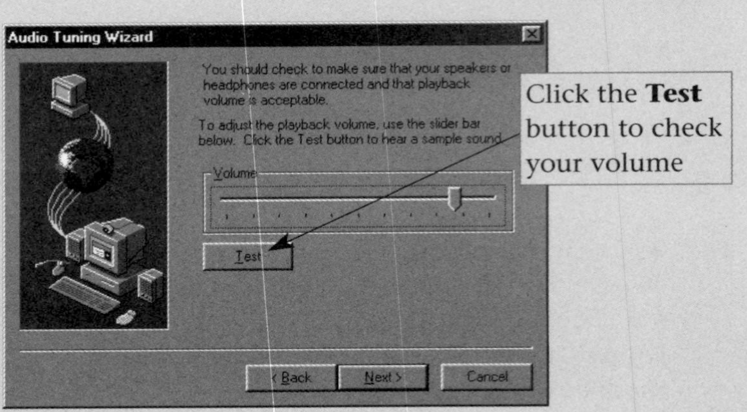

Click the **Test** button to check your volume

Figure 4.7 Check volume

7 The **Recording Test** dialogue box will appear. As NetMeeting tries to establish a recording level, your speakers may make some noises. Read the instructions carefully and speak into your microphone to set the recording level.

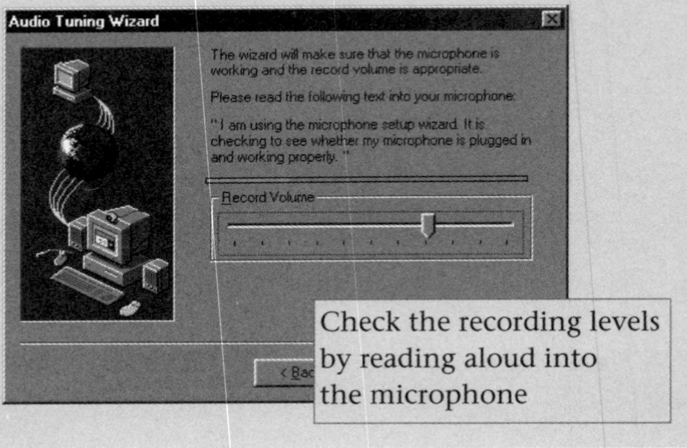

Check the recording levels by reading aloud into the microphone

Figure 4.8 Check recording levels

Information

The green, red and yellow bars on the dialogue box will indicate the recording level and NetMeeting will automatically adjust the level as you speak into the microphone.

You can alter the settings when NetMeeting has finished the setup process, by using the Tools menu.

8 The final dialogue box should indicate that the setup process for NetMeeting has been completed. Click on the **Finish** button to complete the installation.

Figure 4.9 Completing setup

9 The NetMeeting window will now open, but so too will an error message as the program will try to connect to the Microsoft Internet Directory Server, and unless you are already online it won't be able to do so.

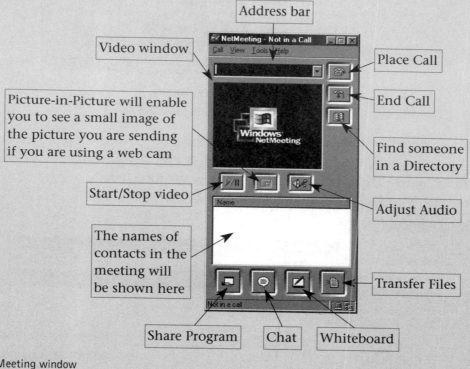

Figure 4.10 NetMeeting window

Having configured and loaded NetMeeting, it's worth spending a few minutes familiarising yourself with the menus and buttons. When you hold your mouse over a button a tool tip will appear telling you what the button does.

You are now ready to begin your first NetMeeting call.

Method

I   You can start a NetMeeting in one of four ways:
  - By selecting **More/Start NetMeeting** from the menu in Messenger.

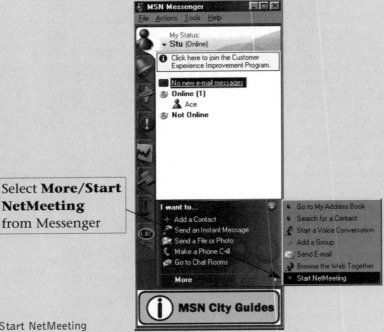

Select **More/Start NetMeeting** from Messenger

Figure 4.11 Select More/Start NetMeeting

  - By clicking the **Place Call** button [image] and entering the e-mail address of your contact or selecting from your address book in the **Place A Call** dialogue box (this will open the Microsoft Internet Directory and list your contacts and their status).
  - By selecting **New Call** from the **Call** menu.

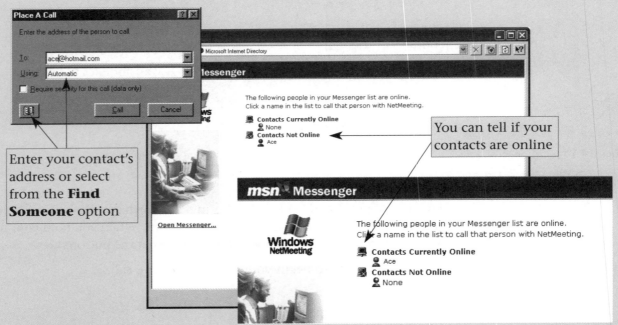

Enter your contact's address or select from the **Find Someone** option

You can tell if your contacts are online

Figure 4.12 Making contact

- By entering one of the following: e-mail address, computer name, telephone number or IP address in the Address bar.

2   Double click the name of the contact you want to hold a NetMeeting with and a message will be sent to them using the Messenger service asking them whether they want to connect with you. If they accept your call, the NetMeeting window will show the people currently in a call. If you are invited to join a NetMeeting by a contact, you will hear a phone ring.

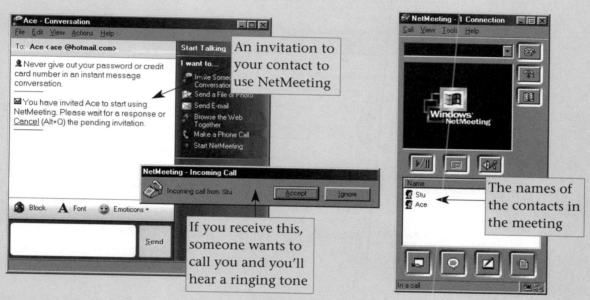

Figure 4.13 Setting up a meeting

3   To chat to your contact click the **Chat** button [image] to open the Chat window. Enter your text in the **Message** box and click the **Send** button [image] to send it.

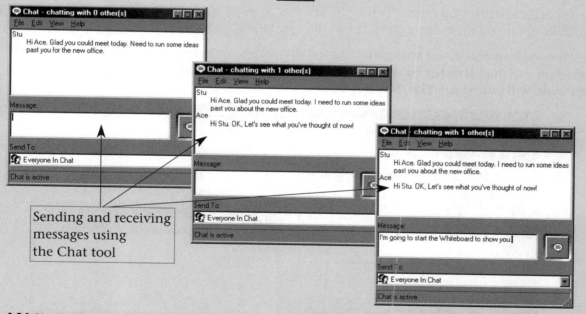

Figure 4.14 Chatting to your contact

Note: If you and your contact in the meeting have speakers and microphones, you can hear each other as well as using text to communicate.

Method

I   Once in the meeting, you can start the **whiteboard** by clicking the Whiteboard button

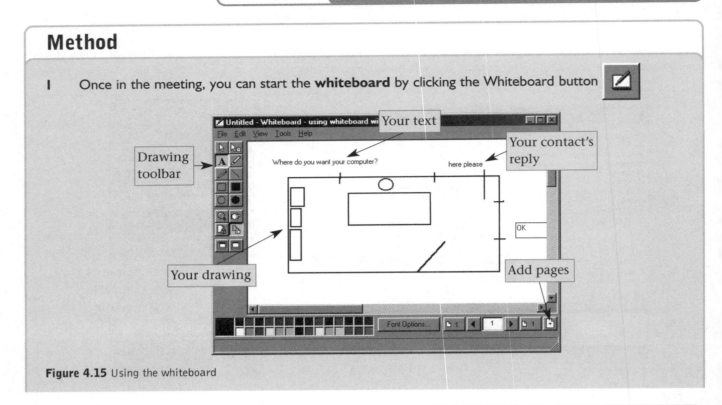

Figure 4.15 Using the whiteboard

Information: About the whiteboard

The Whiteboard window is very similar to Microsoft Paint, but unlike Paint it can have as many pages as you want simply by clicking on the **Insert New Page** button.

You can make a drawing and save it before the meeting to avoid having to draw it in real-time, by using the **File/Save** option on the toolbar. Open the document during the meeting using the **File/Open** option.

Everyone in the meeting can see changes to the drawing as they happen, and can make changes themselves which everyone else will see on their screens. You can add text as well as shapes, etc., and save the drawing using the **File/Save** option.

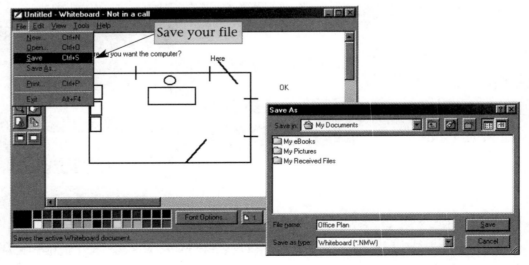

Figure 4.16 Saving your file

Using the **File/Print** option will enable you to print out a copy of the drawing.

If you want to take control of the whiteboard for a while, select the **View/Lock Contents** option or click the **Lock Contents** 🔒 button on the toolbar. With Lock Contents enabled, only you can make changes to the whiteboard until you deselect the option.

| Task 4.4 | **Using NetMeeting to transfer files** |

Method

1   To transfer a file to a contact in the meeting, click the **Transfer Files** button 📄

2   In the **File Transfer** dialogue box, click the **Add Files** button 📄 and browse your hard drive to select the file to send in the **Select Files to Send** dialogue box.

3   Click on **Add** to add the file to the File Transfer window.

4   Click on the **Send** button 📄 to send the file.

5   Close the File Transfer dialogue box when you have received confirmation that the file has been sent.

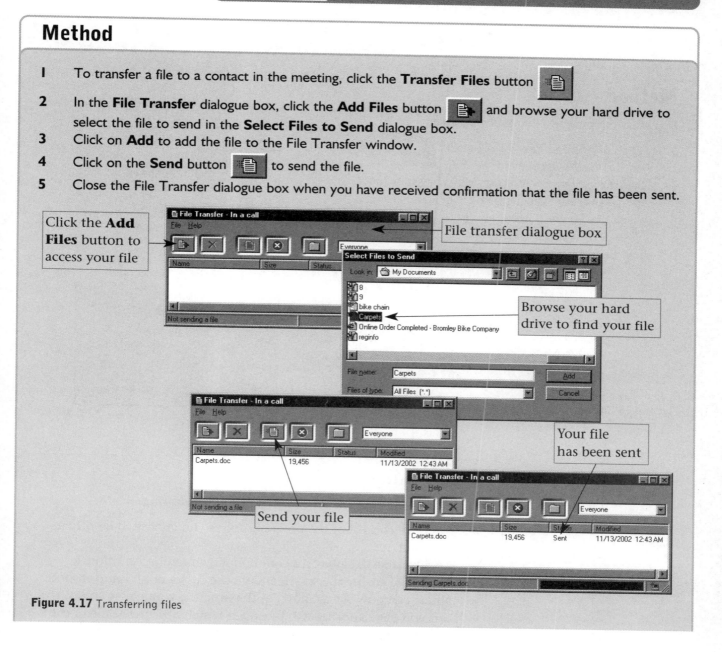

Click the **Add Files** button to access your file

File transfer dialogue box

Browse your hard drive to find your file

Send your file

Your file has been sent

Figure 4.17 Transferring files

As well as the whiteboard facility, you and others in the meeting can share a running program that one or the other of you has open on their screen. You could, for example, take others in the meeting on a guided tour around your web site by running your web browser and sharing your browser window with others. They would see exactly the same images on their screens as you have on yours.

You can also allow others to control the program so that they can edit a document, for example, and this can be saved and printed out later. Even if they don't have the application on their computer, they can still edit the file.

Task 4.5 — Using NetMeeting to share programs

Method

1 Run the program you wish to share.

2 Click the **Share Program** button on the NetMeeting window.

3 Select the program to share from the list in the **Sharing** dialogue box.

4 Click the **Share** button.

5 Your program will appear on everyone's screens.

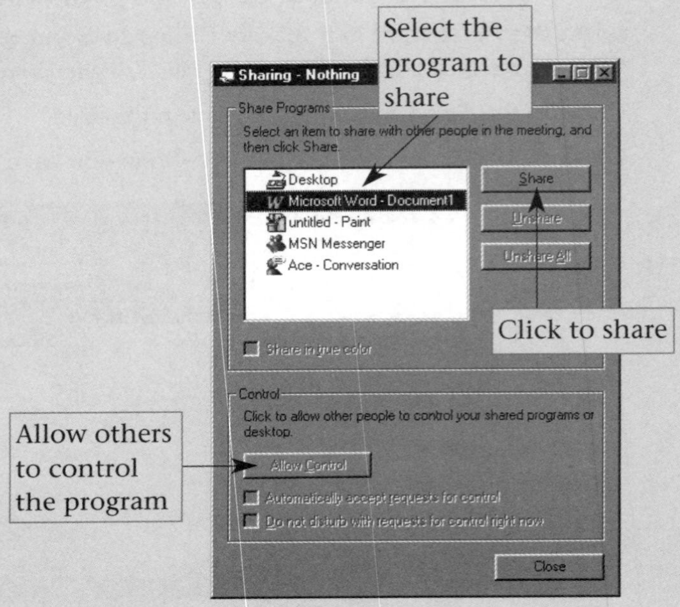

Select the program to share

Click to share

Allow others to control the program

Figure 4.18 Sharing programs

Information

Some pointers to think about when using NetMeeting.

- You have control of the program unless you choose to let others control it.
- It is advisable to agree on a common screen resolution before a meeting to ensure the screen and mouse cursor don't jump around.
- Others can only see as much of the program window as you can, so if you have another window open which obscures some of the shared program window, they will just see blank parts where the windows overlap. You will need to make sure that the running program screen is fully visible by clicking on it, or minimising all other screens.
- Unless you all have fast Internet connections, it may take a little while for the program to be displayed on everyone's screen.

Task 4.6   Allowing others to control your program in NetMeeting

Method

1   In the **Sharing** dialogue box, click **Allow Control**.
2   In the main NetMeeting window, right click the name of a person you want to work in the program, and then click **Grant Control**.

Information

Only one person at a time can control the program.

If **controllable** appears in the title bar of the shared program window, the person who shared the program has control and is allowing others to work in the program. If the mouse pointer has a box with initials, then another meeting participant has control of the program.

You, as the owner of the program, can regain control of the mouse pointer at any time by clicking or pressing any key to take back control.

You can click **Allow Control** at any time during the meeting. When you click it, the button name changes to **Prevent Control**. If you click **Prevent Control**, other participants cannot work in the shared program until you click **Allow Control** again.

Prevent control

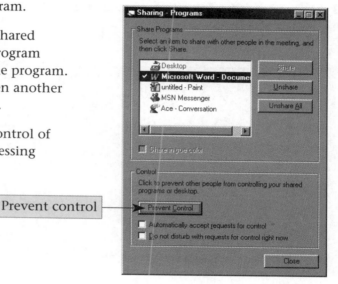

Figure 4.19 Controlling the program

When a participant requests control, NetMeeting displays a message asking your permission. If you want to grant permission automatically, go to the **Sharing** dialogue box and select the **Automatically accept requests for control** check box.

You can accept or reject a request for control

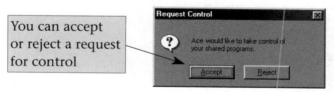

Figure 4.20 Requesting control of program

In NetMeeting you can share not just a running program but also the desktop itself. This is called **desktop sharing**. To share the desktop you need to have no other programs shared and everybody in the meeting will be able to see your entire desktop. If you give control of the desktop to your contacts, they can use this system remotely as though they were sitting in front of it. This is very useful if you have problems with your computer as the technician at the help desk can fix your computer remotely while you watch.

NetMeeting also allows **remote desktop sharing**. To do this, you would call your system from another location, and use the computer as though you were actually sitting in front of it. If you were away from the office, for example, and needed access to files on your office machine you could call your system, browse for the file, and then file transfer it to your current location.

Task 4.7 — Sharing your desktop in NetMeeting

Method

1   You will need to enable remote desktop sharing first. Select **Remote Desktop Sharing** from the **Tools** menu.
2   Follow the instructions given in the Remote Desktop Sharing Wizard.
3   Open the **Sharing** dialogue box and select **Desktop** from the list.
4   Click on the **Share** button.

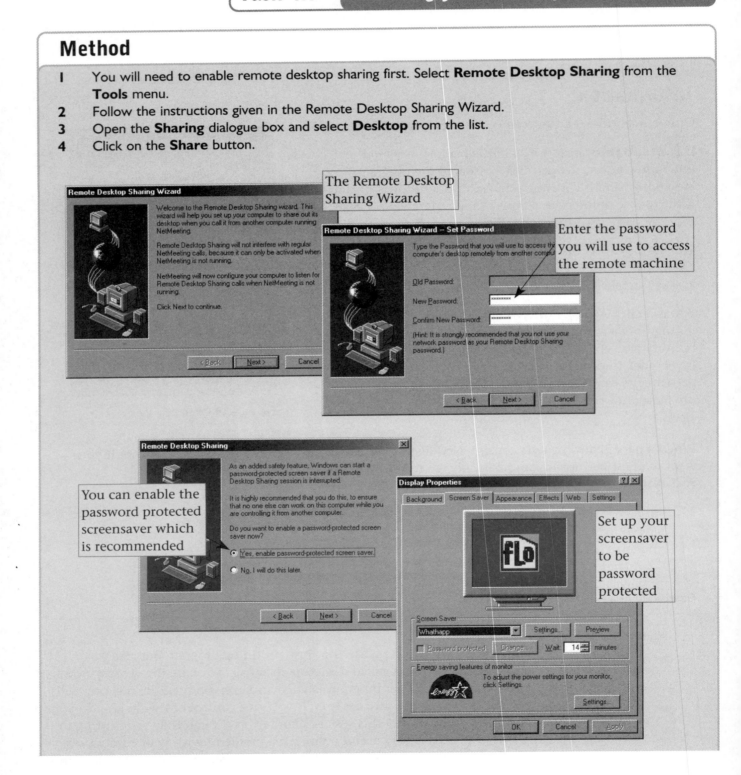

The Remote Desktop Sharing Wizard

Enter the password you will use to access the remote machine

You can enable the password protected screensaver which is recommended

Set up your screensaver to be password protected

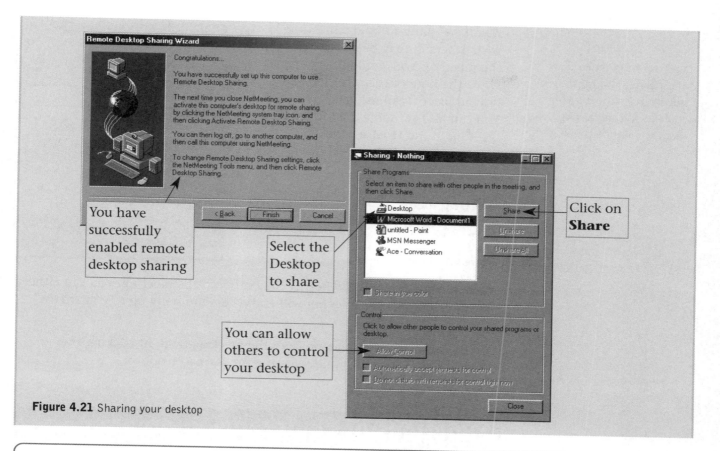

You have successfully enabled remote desktop sharing

Select the Desktop to share

You can allow others to control your desktop

Click on **Share**

Figure 4.21 Sharing your desktop

Information

You can also allow others to control your desktop in the same way as allowing control of a program.

Task 4.8   Ending a NetMeeting call

Method

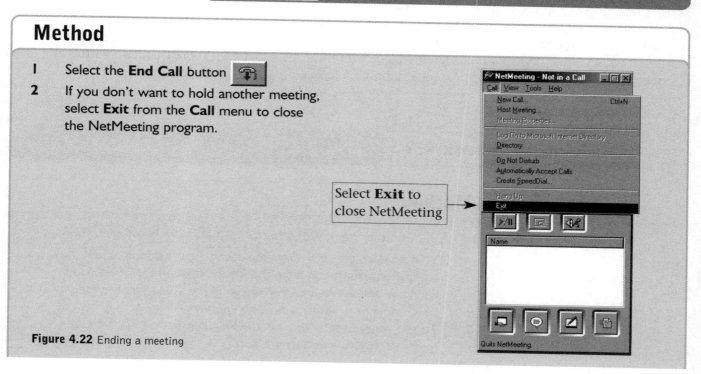

1 Select the **End Call** button

2 If you don't want to hold another meeting, select **Exit** from the **Call** menu to close the NetMeeting program.

Select **Exit** to close NetMeeting

Figure 4.22 Ending a meeting

If you are going to hold a meeting with others, it may be useful to host the meeting. You would let everyone know the time of the meeting, and how to place a call using NetMeeting. You can also set some criteria for the meeting in the **Host a Meeting** dialogue box, which you can access from the **Call/Host Meeting** menu.

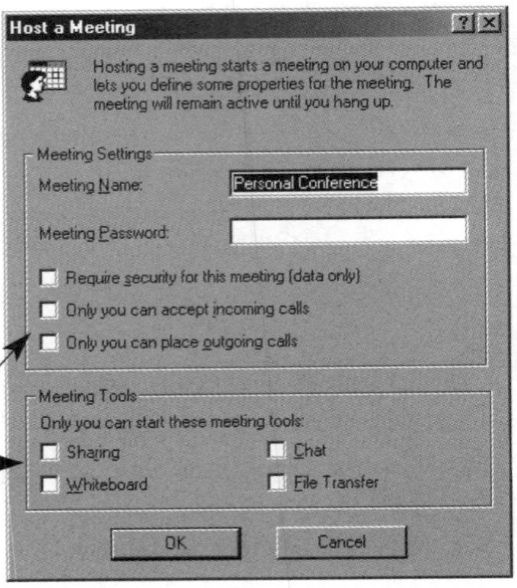

You can set criteria for the meeting

Figure 4.23 Hosting a meeting

As each contact requests whether they can join the meeting, you can either Accept or Ignore. The meeting will end when you hang up as you are the host.

You can also remove someone from the meeting by right clicking the person's name in the list and selecting the **Remove** option.

Functions of conferencing program

If both you and your contact have a video camera or a web cam on your computers, you will be able to see as well as hear or text each other. (In NetMeeting, only the first two people in the call can use this function – see the Information box below.)

Information

NetMeeting only supports audio and video conferencing between the first two people in the call. To have a video/audio conference with more than one other person requires MCUs (multipoint control units) which allow multipoint conferencing, or communication between more than two parties at once (much like a traditional conference call on a telephone).

Task 4.9   Using a video in NetMeeting

Method

1   Click on the **Start Video** button ▶/II in the NetMeeting window. Your contact should be able to receive your video images if they select **Receive** option from the **Tools** menu in their NetMeeting window. You will see a small image of the video you are sending in a small window in your main video window.

2   To see your contact, click on the **Receive** option from the **Tools** menu to receive video from them.

Video/audio conferencing

There are different ways that video conferencing can be used. The hardware and software available will often determine the type of video/audio conference which can be held. The following illustrations show some of the different ways video/audio conferencing can be arranged. They include one-to-one, one-to-many, and many-to-many communication.

Point-to-point call: desktop

This type of video/audio conferencing is achieved with NetMeeting for the first two people in the call.

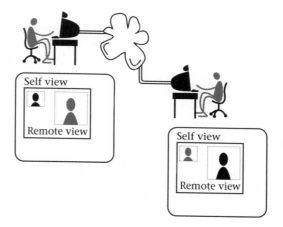

Figure 4.24 Desktop conferencing

Point-to-point call: one to group

This type of video/audio conference would be possible with NetMeeting if the video camera could capture an image of all those in the group or could be swivelled to point to each contact as required.

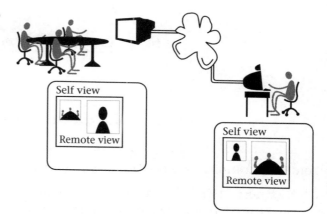

Figure 4.25 One to group conferencing

Point-to-point call: group to group

You would need good video equipment to be able to do this in NetMeeting.

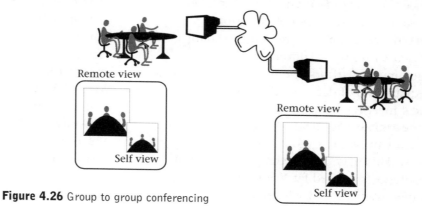

Figure 4.26 Group to group conferencing

For a video/audio conference to be successful, the quality of both is critical. If the video images are jerky and break up, or if the sound is faint and distorted, the participants will not feel as though they are really part of the meeting.

To enable video/audio conferencing across several different sites, **multipoint control units** (**MCU**) would be required to handle data coming from several locations. This would require much more expensive systems and would be used by large organisations and teaching establishments. The following diagram indicates how MCU conferencing might be arranged.

Multipoint call (requires MCU)

Note: MCU stands for multipoint control unit. MCUs vary in their capabilities and in their screen layouts. Some higher end conference room codecs include MCU capability for up to four sites.

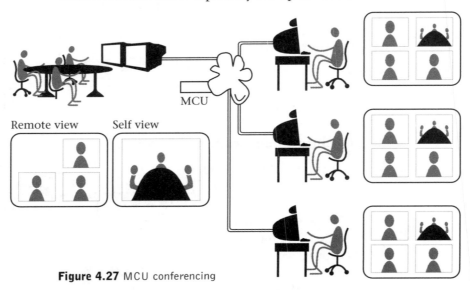

Figure 4.27 MCU conferencing

Some applications for video/audio conferencing technology are:

- **Business** Here video/audio conferencing can be used to hold meetings between people on different sites to save time and money.
- **Teaching and learning** Here whole class teaching can be conducted using video/audio conferencing facilities. This may be used for distance learning or to invite a guest speaker to give a lecture from a remote location.
- **Scientific research** Here you can share and discuss findings at different research establishments without the need to convey large quantities of data or exhibits to a physical meeting.
- **Telemedicine** Medical advice and diagnosis can be carried out using these facilities. This may be especially useful when a consultant is located far from the actual site where their expertise is required.

- **Telecommuting** Working from home can be both a cost-effective and an efficient way of conducting business for both employer and employee. Using video/audio conferencing can keep the two parties in touch with all developments.
- **Judicial applications** Video/audio conferencing is used to good effect by the courts to prevent vulnerable witnesses having to make personal appearances in the courtroom.
- **Surveillance and security** Video/audio conferencing is usually thought of as being a two-way event, but by muting the audio and video it can be used in a one-way monitoring function.

Conferencing in teaching and learning

The following diagrams show how video/audio conferencing can be used to support teaching and learning.

Classroom: guest lecturer or co-instructor

This can be deployed as a single camera installation.

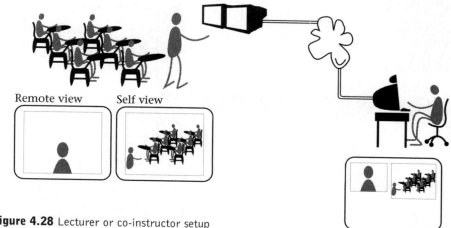

Figure 4.28 Lecturer or co-instructor setup

This setup would enable a guest speaker or instructor to interact with the class and enhance the understanding of the subject matter for students. The speaker may be located in a different area of the country, or even the world, and might not, under normal circumstances, be able to make the expensive and time-consuming journey to talk to the class in person.

Classroom: local and remote classroom

This requires dual-camera installation. The setup would enable two groups in different locations to participate in the lesson.

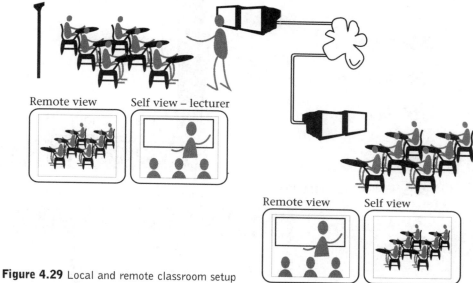

Figure 4.29 Local and remote classroom setup

Data conferencing and chat can also be used to support teaching and learning. The screen capture images that follow show one such example of a **virtual learning environment (VLE)**. This system enables exchange of information and data in real-time, and enables students to access learning remotely from other locations, such as their own homes.

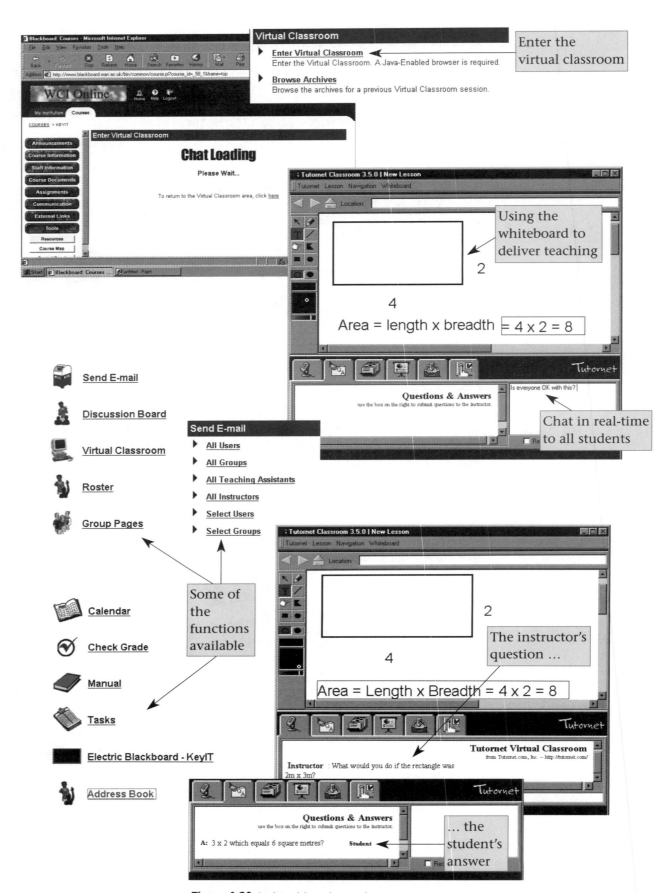

Figure 4.30 A virtual learning environment

→ Practise your skills 1

(You might find it useful to do these exercises with a partner who is also studying this unit.)

1 Ensure that you have a .Net passport. You may need to register for one if you don't have a Hotmail account.
2 Set up your conferencing program.
3 Place a call to your contact and participate in a conference with one other person.
4 Exchange at least three messages using the chat facility in your program.
5 Open the whiteboard and collaboratively produce a drawing of an office layout.
6 Save your whiteboard file to your hard drive with the filename **Office Plan**.
7 Take a screen capture of your desktop showing your whiteboard drawing and print out a copy.
8 End your call and close your conferencing program.

→ Practise your skills 2

1 Access your conferencing program and place a call to your contact.
2 Exchange messages using the chat facility in your conferencing program.
3 Transfer your saved file **Office Plan** to your contact and ask that it be opened in the whiteboard.
4 Collaboratively change some details of the plan displayed in the whiteboard.
5 Save the new plan with the filename **Office Plan 2**.
6 End your call and close your conferencing program.

→ Practise your skills 3

1 Arrange with your contact to place a conferencing call to you.
2 Access your conferencing program and accept the agreed call.
3 Exchange messages using the chat facility in the conferencing program about your experiences of using the program.
4 Take a screen capture of your discussion and print out a copy.
5 End your call and close your conferencing program.

→ Check your knowledge 1

1 What equipment would be required to use the facilities of a conferencing program?
2 In what situations would a conferencing program be useful?
3 List four of the functions of a conferencing program.
4 How could a whiteboard facility be used in a conference?
5 What type of files could you transfer in a conference?
6 What are the advantages of sharing a program during a conference?
7 What would be essential to ensure high quality images and sound in a conference?
8 What would a multipoint control unit (MCU) allow you to do?
9 Identify four uses for audio/video conferencing facilities.
10 How might conferencing be used in teaching and learning?

Consolidation 2

(You might find it helpful to do this exercise with a partner who is also studying this unit.)

1 Load your browser and connect to your ISP.

2 Use advanced search criteria to find information on audio/video conferencing.

3 Bookmark the sites you find and copy and paste the relevant information into a new word processing document. Save the file as **conferencing**.

4 Using a chat program, arrange with your contact a date and time for a conference. Take a screen shot of your chat discussion and print out a copy.

5 Open your e-mail program and, using your ISP account, compose a message to your contact to confirm the arrangements for the conference. Ask your contact to reply to your web-based e-mail account.

6 Set up your ISP account to access your web-based account. Log on to your ISP account and check for new messages.

7 Reply to your contact through your web-based account to remind him or her that you will both need to set your screen resolution at 800×600 for the conference.

8 Load your conferencing program (but don't make a connection) and access the whiteboard facility.

9 Produce a drawing on your whiteboard to illustrate one way of setting up a conference. Save the file as **conference plan**.

10 Close your conference program and load your file compression utility.

11 Create an archive called **conference** and add your two files to the archive. Save the file to your hard drive or an appropriate location.

12 Access your display properties and adjust your display resolution to the agreed figures.

13 Load your conference program at the agreed time and enter into a conference with your contact.

14 Using the chat or audio facility, explain that you will be sending a compressed file with the information about conferencing.

15 Send the file to your contact.

16 Request that your contact decompresses the files and opens the whiteboard drawing in the whiteboard facility.

17 Co-operatively alter the drawing in response to your discussions.

18 Save the new drawing with the filename **conference plans2**.

19 Open the word processed file **conference** and share it with your contact. Make any changes you both feel appropriate and save them.

20 Exit your conference call and close the program.

21 Access the revised files and print out copies.

You will learn to

- Set security features and identify the reasons for using them:
  - ☐ virus protection
  - ☐ firewalls
  - ☐ encryption
  - ☐ digital IDs and signatures
  - ☐ passwords
  - ☐ locks
  - ☐ alerts
- Identify the types of information that may be protected by copyright:
  - ☐ software
  - ☐ music
  - ☐ video
  - ☐ graphics

Security

Computer security is vital to protect your data and personal information. Good security will prevent and detect any unauthorised use of your computer and appropriate prevention methods can stop people without authorisation (sometimes called 'intruders') from accessing your computer or network. With the right security measures on your system, if an intruder does try to access it, you would be able to detect if they were successful or not. If they were successful, you would also be able to find out what they might have done.

It's not just intruders (also known as hackers and crackers) who might be a threat to your files. There are viruses and trojans (more later) which can wreak havoc with your computer as well as making your personal details vulnerable to misuse. If you work in an organisation with a network, you may have sensitive information which needs to be safeguarded from colleagues bent on mischief. A great deal of thought and planning may go into securing your computer from attack, but one threat which is just as ever present as those already mentioned, is the physical theft of the computer and all your files with it.

The Internet has a wealth of information and services to offer the home user as well as businesses, and the value of being able to communicate via e-mail quickly and easily isn't in doubt. We use computers to do our banking and look after our money, and to communicate with others via newsgroups and chat. While you may not feel your data and communications are 'top secret', you don't want anyone reading your e-mails, accessing your personal details, such as financial statements, using your computer to launch attacks on other systems, or sending forged e-mails from your computer.

Intruders are not interested in your identity, they just want to cause mischief by taking control of your system and files. If they use your computer to launch an attack on another system, it hides their true identity and makes it much more difficult for the authorities to trace them. Hackers use 'holes' in computer software to gain access to your machine, and, although software companies will produce patches and security fixes (software code to address the problem), it is still up to you to download the patches and install them to make your computer more secure.

Sometimes the software applications you have installed on your computer may have default settings which allow other users to access your machine unless you change the settings manually to block such access. One example is chat programs which will let others execute commands on your computer.

If you want to keep your computer as safe as possible it is worth taking every precaution to ensure that the only person that can access its system is you!

Viruses and trojans

One of the best known threats to your files and your computer itself is a virus. These malicious programs are buried inside something which looks innocent and safe, but once unleashed can cause havoc with your data. They can hitch a ride in an e-mail attachment or on a downloaded file from the Internet. Whichever way they travel, it is vital to have your virus checker installed, up-dated regularly and active. Most commercial anti-virus software will have features that you can set to monitor all files passing through your Internet connection, and if they detect a virus they will alert you and eliminate it.

Viruses come in many forms and can cause worldwide problems, as witnessed by the spread of the 'I Love You' virus, discovered on 4 May 2000, which caused many systems administrators to close down their whole network. A very high-risk threat in November 2002 was a virus called 'Bugbear', which is a mass-mailing worm (sends e-mails to everyone in the infected computer's address book) and potentially allows unauthorised access to the infected computer.

The screen capture images which follow, taken from the Symantec (a well-known anti-virus software developer) web site, gives details of the 'I Love You' virus which caused so many problems in 2000 and the virus threats in November 2002. This type of information is available from many commercial anti-virus software vendors and will give details of the type and severity of the virus.

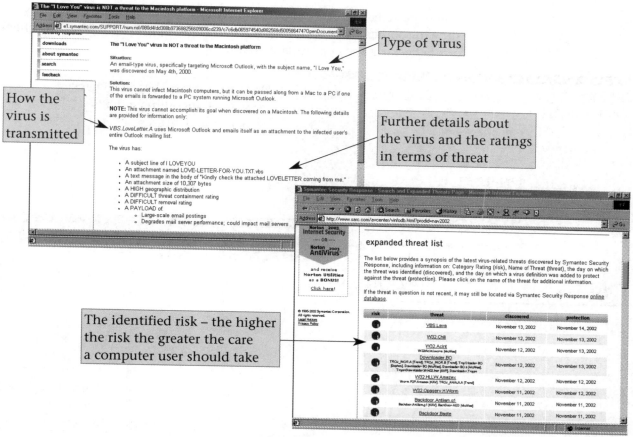

Figure 5.1 Virus threat details

The term virus is used to cover a variety of digital organisms:

- **Virus** is a program that infects another program, boot sector, partition sector or document that supports macros. Some viruses can be fairly harmless whilst others can cause a great deal of damage to data or a hard drive.

- **Trojans** (named after the Trojan horses of Greek mythology) can often appear as a useful or amusing program, but once installed on your machine it can allow a hacker to gain access to your computer and the hard drive.

- **Bombs** sit quietly on your computer until a preset event or time occurs to activate it and unleash destruction on your hard drive.

- **Worms** are programs that copy themselves independently and clog up your hard drive. Worms can be transported by e-mail or floppy disk, and could compromise the security of the computer.

- **Hoaxes** are often similar to a chain letter – they can cause worry, but little damage to your machine.

- **Jokes** generally cause silly screen-savers to pop up unexpectedly, or similar harmless activities.

The best way to protect your computer from these nasties is to install a good anti-virus program which will monitor and scan all downloaded files for any potential threat. Installing such a program isn't enough, however. It is important to keep your virus definitions (which recognise the virus) up-to-date by connecting to your program developer's web site regularly and downloading the latest data. New viruses are being developed all the time, and updating should be done at least once a week.

These are screen shots from a commercially available anti-virus utility showing some of the options available. These options can be set by checking or unchecking the appropriate boxes.

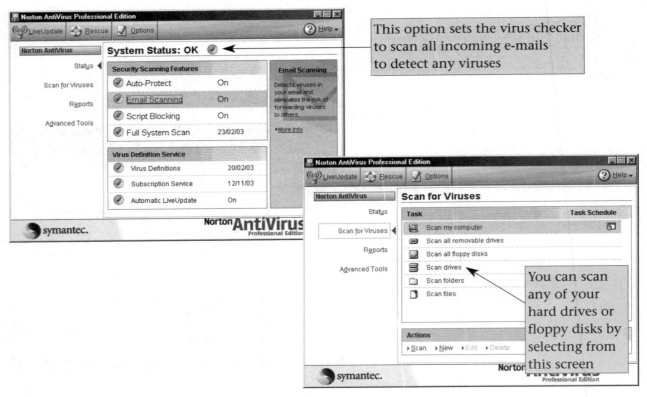

Figure 5.2 An anti-virus utility

All viruses can be potentially harmful, but the most alarming are the **trojans**, which usually work by hiding on your hard drive and setting themselves up to run each time you start up your computer. Once up and running, they will open a back door to your system through which a hacker can communicate with your machine. Sitting quietly in the background, the hacker will be able to take control of your computer, download files, alter files and settings, and sniff out passwords stored by the operating system, such as your ISP logon password. Some more advanced trojans have a key logger, which allows the hacker to 'see' the letters you type, including your username, passwords, and any credit card details you enter. A good anti-virus utility should be able to detect and eliminate a trojan before it can settle onto your hard drive.

Information

There are several thousands of known viruses, and, although you can detect and destroy them with an anti-virus utility when they try to infect your computer, the virus itself can't be destroyed and lives on out in the Internet. In November 2002, Symantec, a well-known anti-virus software developer, listed 62,328 virus definitions on its web site.

In Section 2 there are details on setting your safety levels in Internet Explorer. Using this facility you can set up your browser to disable the downloading of files altogether, which will prevent any viruses being transmitted with downloaded files.

Method

1   Select **Internet Options** from the **Tools** menu.
2   Select the **Security** tab.
3   Click the **Custom Level** button.
4   Scroll down the options to the **Downloads** section and check the **File download/Disable** option.
5   Click the **OK** button twice.

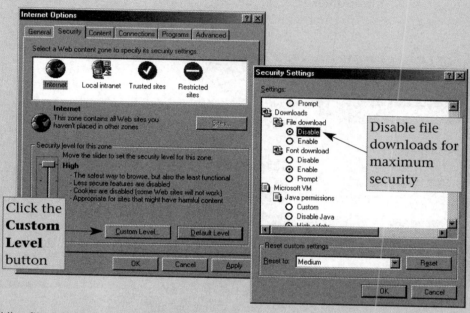

Figure 5.3 Disabling file download

Information

There are several other options to change security settings using this process, such as disabling font downloads, disabling active scripting and setting the user authentication.

Firewalls

When you connect to the Net there is always a chance that you may inadvertently download a file with a virus or allow a hacker to access your computer through your connection. However if you are using your phone line at home and your virus checking software regularly, you are fairly safe from attack. With the increasing use of cable and broadband connections, which are permanently connected to the Internet, your computer is much more vulnerable to attack. Firewalls are one possible means of protection against such intrusion. They provide a system that prevents unauthorised access to a computer over a network, such as the Internet. Firewalls can be either hardware or software. Business will tend to use a hardware firewall, whereas a home user would probably use software.

A firewall will check every bit of data that goes in and out of your computer, to ensure that only acceptable data ends up on your machine. Firewalls may also detect viruses, which can save a lot of problems if you forget to update your virus checker. The difference between these two types of programs is becoming increasingly blurred, as they are being developed to provide both types of protection.

The screen shots show a software firewall program which can be downloaded from the Internet. With this type of program you can set your security levels with various options and completely lock your computer to any Internet activity if a period of time has passed since any activity was monitored. This can be very useful if you have a permanent connection to the Internet which you may not be accessing all the time.

Figure 5.4 A firewall program

When downloading is complete you can install and set up the program to monitor any attempts at intrusion while you surf.

Encryption

Encryption is used to scramble data so that it becomes difficult to understand and interpret. There can't be many students who haven't used a basic encryption system to pass messages to friends in class, such as changing every letter in a message to a letter five places further down the alphabet, making the word 'hello' appear as 'ojqqt'. To unscramble this code, you would need to know the secret system used to scramble the word. Unscrambling text is called decryption. Text that has been encrypted is called **cyphertext**.

E-mail is a quick and easy way to communicate with friends and colleagues, but it isn't really strictly private. Your e-mail could be forwarded to someone else, or it could be intercepted and read without your knowledge, or your e-mail could remain on a backup system, your network for example, waiting for someone other than the recipient to read it. This is why it is becoming increasingly popular to encrypt e-mails to ensure they remain private.

There are two methods of encryption: symmetric key encryption and public key encryption.

Symmetric key encryption

The same key is used to both encrypt and decrypt the message. It is very similar to the code used by students in the classroom. A computer will have a secret key (code) that it can use to encrypt a packet of information before it is sent over a network to another computer, and, as long as the recipient's computer has the same secret key installed, the message can be decrypted. To anyone else without the key, the message would just appear as gobble-de-gook.

Public key encryption

A combination of a private key and a public key is used. The private key is known only to you (or rather to your computer) and the public key is available to anyone who wants to send you secure information. The two keys are linked together with a mathematical algorithm, a complex mathematical relationship. The message is encrypted using the public key, and decrypted using the private key. Only you, the keeper of the private key, can decrypt the message.

If two computer users want to exchange encrypted messages, they would both need their own private keys and need to have given each other their public keys. For example, if Jack wants to send an encrypted message to Jill, he uses her public key. Jill would then use her private key to decrypt the message. The computer carries out the encryption using a special software program.

One of the best-known encryption utilities is PGP (Pretty Good Privacy), developed by Phil Zimmerman in the early 1990s. This encryption program is so effective that some governments are very concerned about its use.

A different approach is required to implement public key encryption on a large scale, such as that required by a commercial web site. In this case **digital certificates** are used. A digital certificate is an attachment to an electronic message to verify that the sender of the message is who he or she claims to be. It will also enable the recipient to encode a reply. A **certificate authority (CA)** will issue a digital certificate containing the public key of the person or organisation applying for the certificate, together with other information such as an expiry date and a serial number. The person receiving the encrypted message uses the CA's public key to decrypt the digital certificate, verifying that the CA has issued it. The receiver can then access the sender's public key contained within the certificate and use it to encrypt the reply.

One well-known implementation of public key encryption is the **Secure Sockets Layer (SSL)**, which recently became part of an overall security protocol known as **Transport Layer Security (TLS)**.

SSL is a protocol, originally developed by Netscape for transmitting private documents over the Internet. SSL uses a public key to encrypt data that is transferred over an SSL connection, making it almost impossible for someone else to capture and make use of the information unless they have the private key to decrypt the data. This protocol is used by web sites to ensure the safety of confidential information, such as your credit or debit card number, in exchanges over the Internet. Both Internet Explorer and Netscape Navigator support SSL and web addresses for sites offering secure data transmission should start with 'https://' rather than the plain 'http://' as shown in this example:

Figure 5.5 SSL secured web site address

When you buy your new CD or book over the Net, your financial transaction will be secured by SSL. In fact, many online purchases and monetary transactions are secured using this protocol, making using the Internet for business more secure.

There is also another way of ensuring that the information you receive comes from a trusted source – **authentication**. Often encryption and authentication work together to create a secure environment.

Authentication of a person, organisation or information can be by:

- **Password** Your user name and password provides probably the most common form of authentication. Most of us will have received the warning informing us that the password we entered is incorrect, usually because we've entered it wrongly! The site you are accessing will check your details with a secure file to see if they match before it will allow you to enter.
- **Access token** Examples of these are smart cards used with a smart card reader attached to the computer.
- **Digital signatures** These use public key encryption systems to generate a digital ID which can be used to prove your identity.
- **Biometrics** Your personal characteristics are used to identify you. Fingerprints, for example, are a unique identifier. Other areas of biometric technology are iris recognition, hand geometry, palm prints and voice.

→ Check your knowledge 1

1 Are hackers the only threat to the security of your computer?
2 Name three different types of viruses, and describe the effect they may have.
3 What should you do with your virus checker on a regular basis?
4 Why might a broadband connection to the Net be more vulnerable to attack than a connection via your phone line at home?
5 Why might you install a firewall?

6   What are the two types of encryption in common use?

7   Where would you obtain a digital certificate?

8   How would you know if a web site you were visiting was using SSL?

9   Why might you want to encrypt your e-mail messages?

10 What type of key would your contact need to send you an encrypted message?

Digital IDs (digital certificates) and digital signatures

As more people send information by e-mail, it is becoming increasingly important that your e-mails can't be read by anyone other than your recipient. A system to ensure that no one can pretend to be you and send information under your name, which may be false or misleading, is vital in today's business world. This can be done using **digital IDs** (also called **digital certificates**). Digital IDs are made up of a public key, a private key and a **digital signature**. When you use your digital ID to sign your message, you are adding a digital signature and public key too.

Using digital IDs in Outlook Express can prove your identity in electronic transactions, a bit like using your passport when you change foreign currency. If you have a digital ID, other people will be able to use your public key to encrypt messages to you, which you will be able to decrypt with your private key. You can also use your recipients' digital IDs to encrypt your replies to keep them from prying eyes using their public keys. Your recipients can decrypt the messages using their private keys.

Digital IDs are issued by independent certification authorities, which will need to verify that you are who you say you are! You do this by completing a form on their web site with your personal details and they will then send you instructions on installing your digital ID. You can then use this to 'sign' your e-mails and ensure that your messages are secure.

Task 5.2	Obtaining a digital ID and adding it to your e-mail account

Method

1   Log on to a certification authority web site and obtain a digital ID. You will need to follow the instructions given on the web site. A list of links can be obtained from Microsoft Outlook Express Digital ID web site.

2   Start a new message and select the **Digitally Sign** option from the **Tools** menu.

3   Enter your message and send it in the usual way.

The screen capture images show the process to register for a digital ID from a certificate authority (www.thawte.com).

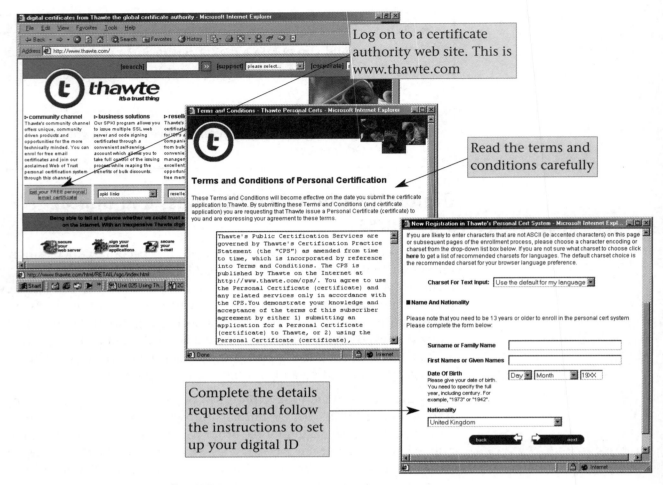

Figure 5.6 Registering for a digital ID

Information

Outlook Express automatically adds your digital ID to your e-mail account when you send your first digitally signed message.

Having obtained your digital ID you can send digitally signed e-mails, which will allow your contact to verify your identity.

Task 5.3   Sending digitally signed e-mail

Method

1   Start a new message.
2   Enter your contact's e-mail address and compose your message in the usual way.
3   To digitally sign the message, on the **Tools** menu click **Digitally Sign**.
4   Send your e-mail in the usual way.

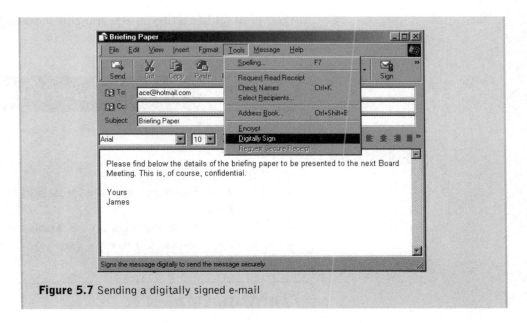

Figure 5.7 Sending a digitally signed e-mail

To send an encrypted message you must have the recipient's digital ID entered in your address book. By default, Outlook Express automatically adds digital IDs to your address book when you receive digitally signed mail, unless you have turned off this option when you will need to add the contact's digital ID manually.

Information

To enable automatic entry of digital IDs in your address book,

1 Select **Tools/Options** and click the **Security** tab.
2 Click the **Advanced** button.
3 In the **Advanced Security Settings** dialogue box, check the **Add senders' certificates to my address book** option.

Task 5.4 ┃ **Adding a contact's digital ID to your address book manually**

Method

1 Open the digitally signed message.
2 Select **Properties** from the **File** menu.
3 Select the **Security** tab and click the **Add digital ID to the address book** button.

Information

When a contact in your address book has a digital ID, a red rosette is added to their details.

If your contact has a digital ID, you can send encrypted messages to them using their public key.

Task 5.5 — Sending an encrypted message

Method

1 Start a new message.
2 Enter your contact's e-mail address and compose your message in the usual way.
3 To encrypt the message, on the **Tools** menu click **Encrypt**.
4 Send your e-mail in the usual way.

Information

These icons will be shown by your messages in the message list.

The message is digitally signed and unopened.

The message is encrypted and unopened.

The message is digitally signed, encrypted, and unopened.

The message is digitally signed and has been opened.

The message is encrypted and has been opened.

The message is digitally signed and encrypted, and has been opened.

Information

You can check the validity of a digitally signed message using revocation checking. This can be accessed through the **Tools/ Options/Advanced** settings. Revocation checking is only available when you are online, when Outlook Express will request information about the digital ID from the appropriate certification authority.

Buying online

Security of personal information is one of the greatest concerns that people have about shopping online, or transacting any other business via the Net. Credit card fraud is one of the biggest worries for many people who may otherwise use the Net for commerce. However, taking reasonable, common sense precautions and using the security measures available should make buying online as safe as handing your credit card to the waiter in a restaurant.

Some rules to help:

- Keep records of transactions, such as e-mail confirmation of order.
- Provide only the minimum information required. Some of the fields in a personal information form are not compulsory, so only complete those that are.

- Always check that the web site is secure. You can tell if it is by the closed lock icon in Internet Explorer 🔒 (or the unbroken key icon in Netscape Navigator) which appears on your status bar. If you set your Internet Options to warn you if you enter or leave a secure site, you will see alerts similar to those shown below. (This setting is the default setting so you shouldn't need to change it.) As your data is encrypted when you send it to a secure site, your details should be safe.

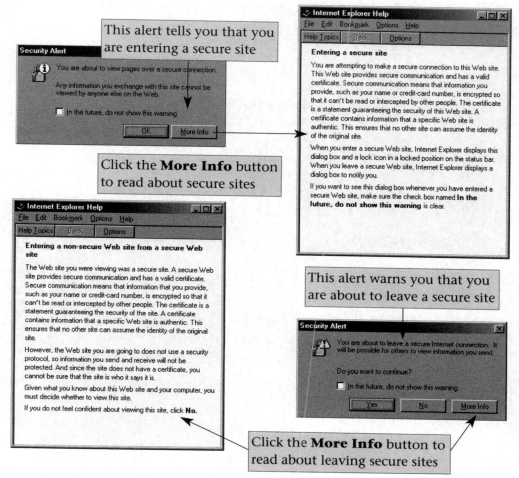

Figure 5.8 Secure site alerts

Digital certificates are used to ensure the security of your information. A web site will have a digital certificate with the public key posted on it. When you access the site and download the certificate, you can then exchange information using SSL technology. The web site owner can decrypt your details with the private key, ensuring that your encrypted data has not been compromised.

You can change how Internet Explorer and Outlook Express handles these certificates, for example to enable checking for publisher's certification revocation.

Task 5.6 Enabling security options in Outlook Express

Method

1. Access the **Options** dialogue box through the **Tools/Options** menu.
2. Select the **Security** tab.
3. Click the **Advanced** button and select the options you want.
4. Click on **OK**.
5. Click on **Apply** to implement the changes.

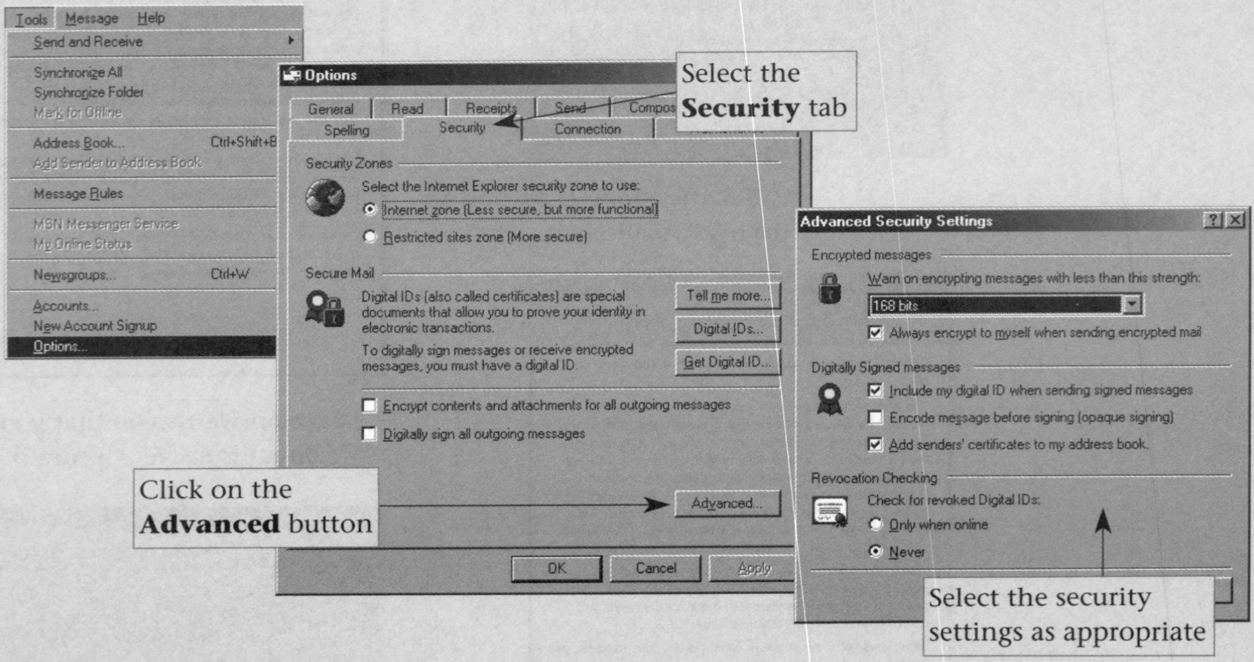

Figure 5.9 Security options

The certificates on your computer are shared by both Outlook Express and Internet Explorer. The method below shows how to view these certificates in Internet Explorer.

Task 5.7 Viewing security options in Internet Explorer

Method

1. In Internet Explorer, select **Internet Options** on the **Tools** menu.
2. Select the **Content** tab.
3. Under **Certificates**, click the **Certificates** button or the **Publishers** button to view the list of current certificates.

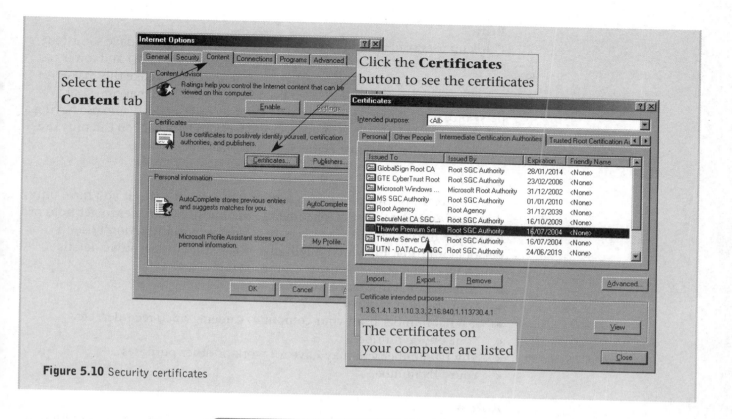

Figure 5.10 Security certificates

> ## Information
>
> There are several certificate authorities on the Web.

Passwords

Passwords can be very effective tools to enable or restrict access to a wide range of resources and services, including web sites, e-mail, files, your desktop, even your computer itself. It is one way to protect your data, your personal information and your peace of mind! A password is a simple system to do all this, but the responsibility is yours to use passwords that are not easy to guess and to keep them safe from prying eyes.

A good password is something that cannot be found in readily available password dictionaries, or by cracking programs and password sniffers (which can capture data from information packets as they travel over the Net).

Some rules to follow when using passwords:

Rule 1

Don't use passwords that consist of easily obtainable personal information, such as your date of birth, your phone number, your own name or, for that matter, your pet's name. Some examples of poor passwords are:

- Any word in a dictionary, in any language
- Any name or nickname
- Names of places, such as cities, countries, forests, mountains
- Titles of films, books, music
- Religious figures, places or events
- Special numbers, like your date of birth, your car registration number, your postcode
- Anything which might be found in a list.

Rule 2

Think up passwords which have at least six characters which have some letters and numbers mixed together, for example 3fr&7nm£ or upper and lower case letters and characters mixed together. A random password like this makes it much harder for someone else to guess. Check, before you make up your password, what the maximum length of a password can be. It's no use having a long complicated password of fifteen numbers and letters if you can only use eight – especially if the first eight characters spell out a word.

Rule 3

Use a different password for each service you register with. If you have only one password, it's too easy for someone of doubtful character to get hold of it and use it to access all your accounts. Most importantly, don't use personal information which might give out even more sensitive details which would be open to misuse. Some examples are:
- Your national insurance number
- Your passport number
- A serial number from your computer, camera, video recorder, etc.
- Your phone number
- Any ID number you may have for work or other purposes
- Your PIN number.

Rule 4

You could find that you end up with quite a number of passwords for different sites, etc. and it gets increasingly difficult to remember which one to use for each purpose. There are programs available which will save and manage your passwords for you, but sometimes old-fashioned pen and pencil is just as easy. If that is the case, make sure that anyone seeing them can't guess what they are, just as you would with your PIN number for your credit or debit card.

Rule 5

Never tell anyone your password.

Rule 6

Change your passwords regularly, especially for sensitive sites such as your online bank. How often you change it depends on how often you use it and who may have seen it, or seen the keystrokes you make as you enter it.

If you are working on a network, you will probably have to enter your password to log on. Every user will be allowed to access only certain parts of the data available, and this will be controlled centrally by the operating system. Users will have passwords which they will enter when they log on to the system to be able to access programs and data. The operating system will check that the password is correct and then allow the user to begin using the software and information available to them. A typical log on screen is shown below:

Figure 5.11 A log on screen

As you surf the Net, you will no doubt come across sites that require you to sign in with your user name or e-mail address, and your password.

Register as a new user >>

or

Enter registered user details below

Email Address: [   ]

Password: [   ] It doesn't matter if you use capital letters or not.

Login >>

Forgotten password >>

Change password >>

Please review the **terms and conditions**

Figure 5.12 Signing in

This will allow you to access parts of the site not otherwise available, for example, or pick up your web-based e-mail. This is your best defence against anyone else accessing your personal account without authority. With this protection comes some responsibilities and it is important that you choose and safeguard your passwords carefully. A web site can only check that a password entered is one which it can accept; it cannot tell whether the person entering it is you!

There are other passwords too that can keep your data safe. You will have a password to log on to Windows when you first start up your computer and you can set a password to activate when your screensaver kicks in.

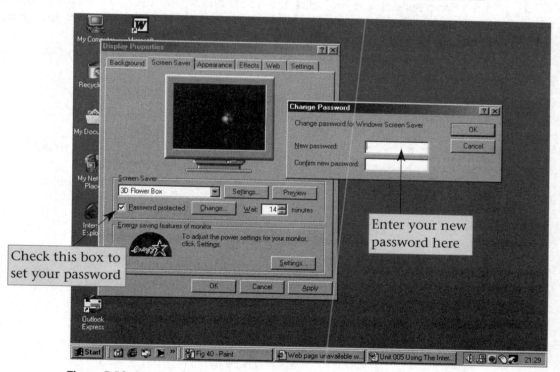

Figure 5.13 Setting your password

You will probably use a password to connect to your ISP. You can check the 'Save password' box (see figure 5.14), but it would be much safer to be prompted to enter it every time you want to log on.

You can password protect your files, such as the sensitive word processed report you have just completed, or the budget forecast you've calculated, which you would rather didn't become public knowledge until an appropriate time.

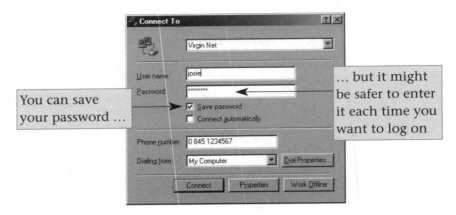

You can save your password …

… but it might be safer to enter it each time you want to log on

Figure 5.14 Enter your password every time you log on

Task 5.8 — Setting a password option in a Word document

Method

1 Open the document.
2 Select the **Save As** option in the **File** menu.
3 In the **Save As** dialogue box, click the **Tools** button and select the **General Options** from the menu.
4 In the **Save** dialogue box which appears, select either the **Password to open** option or the **Password to modify** option. Enter your password. Click on **OK**.
5 In the **Confirm Password** box, type in the password again and click on **OK**.
6 Click on **Save**.

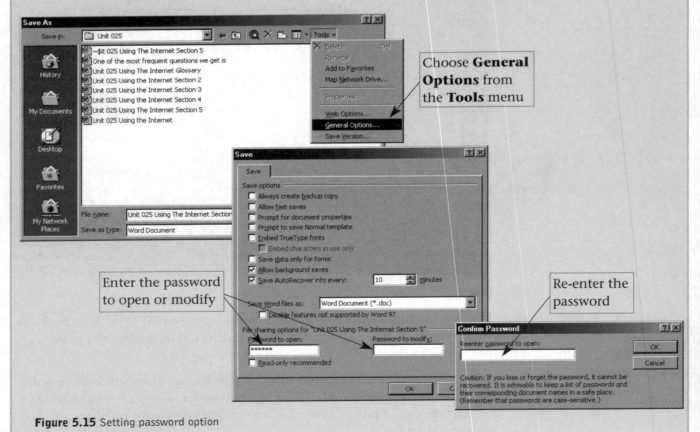

Choose **General Options** from the **Tools** menu

Enter the password to open or modify

Re-enter the password

Figure 5.15 Setting password option

Locks

Locks have always provided one way of securing your valuables, and with your valuable data at risk, locks for your computer can protect your data and your peace of mind.

Computer locks can be hardware, much like the lock you would use to keep your bicycle safe, or software, which protects your data from inside the computer case.

Hardware locks can be used to prevent unauthorised access to your floppy disk drive or your CD-ROM drive, for example. These are often in the form of blanking plates which will mount onto the face of your drive. There are also locks which can be attached to your PC and secured to something too heavy or difficult to move, to prevent theft. No amount of software security will help if your computer is stolen!

One lock many computer users will be familiar with is the write-protect notch on the floppy disk, which prevents the contents being overwritten

Software locks can be used to allow or restrict access to certain functions of the computer. They can vary from locking the mouse to prevent unauthorised use of your computer, to complex programs which can 'hide' files, programs, drives and functions, as well as restricting the ability to change, delete, move and load programs. Most network administrators will be able to allow or restrict access rights to certain facilities and functions through the operating system.

The following screen capture images show some commercially available software which will enable you to lock various parts of your computer.

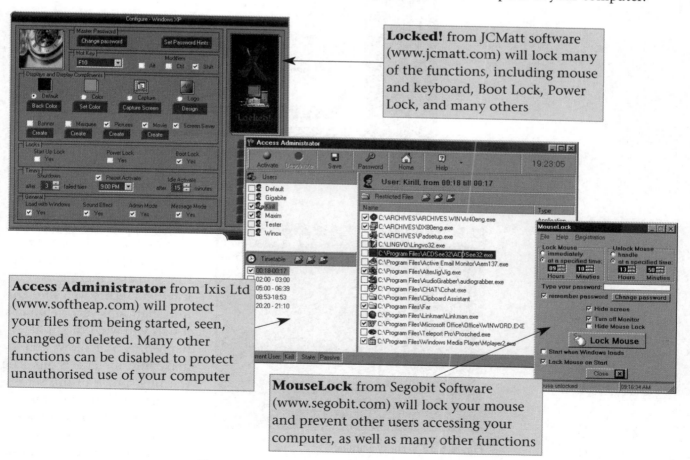

Locked! from JCMatt software (www.jcmatt.com) will lock many of the functions, including mouse and keyboard, Boot Lock, Power Lock, and many others

Access Administrator from Ixis Ltd (www.softheap.com) will protect your files from being started, seen, changed or deleted. Many other functions can be disabled to protect unauthorised use of your computer

MouseLock from Segobit Software (www.segobit.com) will lock your mouse and prevent other users accessing your computer, as well as many other functions

Figure 5.16 Examples of software locks

One familiar example of a software lock is the password protected screen saver you may have enabled to activate after a period away from your computer.

In some versions of the Windows operating system, you can lock the keyboard using the Windows logo key ( ) + L as long as the account has a password associated with it.

Alerts

An **alert** is an audible or visual alarm that signals an error, represents a warning of some sort, or informs you of an event. Anyone who has used a computer for any length of time will certainly have seen alerts on the screen at one time or another. Some can be as simple as a suggestion that the printer may not be turned on; others may give you a timely warning that a new virus has been discovered and updating your virus checker is advisable. Some web sites offer an alert service to keep you informed about the latest news, or that you've forgotten Auntie Maud's birthday!

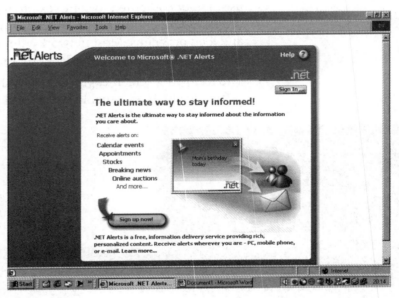

Figure 5.17 Alerts

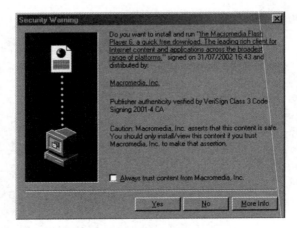

Figure 5.18 Security warning

Earlier in this section, screen capture images of security alerts are shown to warn you that you are entering or leaving a secure web site. This information is very helpful as it tells you what might be happening and allows you to make informed decisions. The warning shown in this screen capture asks whether you want to install some software. It is always worth reading these alerts carefully to check what you need to do.

Some programs, such as Microsoft's Outlook, can be set to alert you to an event or remind you to do something, as shown in these screen capture images. These can also play a reminder sound to make sure you don't miss something important.

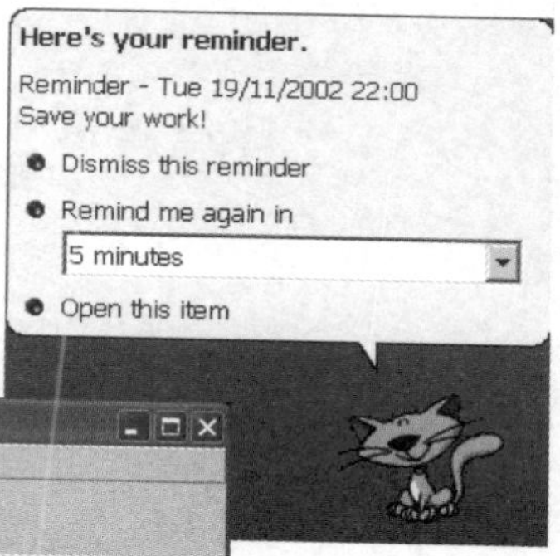

Here's your reminder.

Reminder - Tue 19/11/2002 22:00
Save your work!

● Dismiss this reminder

● Remind me again in
  5 minutes

● Open this item

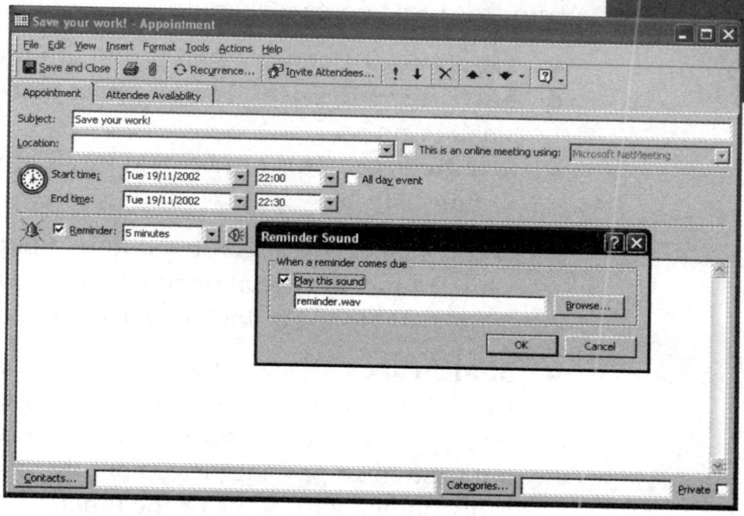

Figure 5.19 A reminder

→ Check your knowledge 2

1 What will make up a digital ID?

2 How might you be able to tell if your contact has a digital ID?

3 How would you digitally sign your messages?

4 Identify two safeguards you can take to ensure security of transactions over the Net.

5 List the rules to follow when using passwords.

6 If your friend was using the password ManUtd to access her online bank, what would your advice be?

7 List all the occasions you can remember in the last week when you have used a password.

8 When did you last change a password?

9 Why might a network administrator want to use software locks?

10 What is an alert?

Copyright

Copyright is a law that protects the work of an author or artist. Copyright information cannot be used without asking the author for permission. The Copyright Design and Patents Act 1988 governs the law of copyright.

Software programs have a copyright. It is illegal to copy them without permission and you may have to pay a large fine if you are caught. This is because software is very costly to produce as it takes many hundreds of hours of developers' time to write the programs. When you buy software you buy a licence to use it, not the software itself, which is why it is illegal to copy someone else's software to load on your own machine. An organisation called FAST (Federation Against Software Theft) has been set up by the major software developers to detect and stop illegal copying of software.

There are different licences available and you should always read the small print to check what you can do. Some of the licences available are:

- **Single-user licence**   This is only for use on one machine at a time.
- **Multi-user licence**   For use on an agreed number of machines, e.g. in a small business.
- **Site licence**   This can be used by all users within a site, e.g. in a college or university.

Some software can be used on a different basis, such as shareware or freeware. Non-commercial organisations or individuals who are not as concerned about loss of income have often developed this software.

- **Shareware**   This is usually distributed free, and can often be found on the CDs distributed with computer magazines or on web sites. Quite often you can use the software for a specified period of time to try it out, but then must pay a fee if you decide to keep it. Sometimes this software is distributed with some of the functions disabled or it may have an expiry time set within the program, such as a twenty-use-only facility.
- **Freeware**   This can be distributed and used freely without any charge. The copyright of the software usually remains with the originator, but you can use it without having to pay. This type of software often consists of small utility programs and can also be found on web sites and cover discs.
- **Music**   Computers today can download, play and burn music files onto CD. Music is also copyright and there has been a lot of information in the computer press about the illegal copying and selling of music files. One web site doing this was closed down, so it is being taken very seriously.
- **Video**   Video is protected by copyright laws in the same way as other media, with the copyright resting with the producer and director. With modern computer technology, it is possible to copy whole films to a recordable DVD and, as with music, this too could be a breach of copyright without permission from the copyright holders. This principle also applies to videos recorded from the television.
- **Graphics**   Images can be easily captured or scanned using computer technology. This is also information which is protected by copyright. If you use any images from other people you could be infringing copyright law if you don't seek permission or check with the small print that it is OK to do so.
- **Data**   There is a market for personal details that can be used by direct marketing companies to mail shot people on the lists with offers and other information. This could be by snail mail or through your e-mail inbox. All data is protected.

Information

The information contained on many web sites may also be copyright – you would need to check the small print to see.

→ Practise your skills 1

1 Log on to your ISP and search for a web site which will give you information about the latest virus threat.
2 Make notes of the information you find.
3 Search for another web site giving similar details and check if the same virus threat is identified.
4 Add to your notes any further information you can find from the site.
5 Run your anti-virus utility to check your computer is free from infection.

→ Practise your skills 2

1 Access your Internet Explorer options and note down your advanced security settings.
2 Take a screen shot and print out a copy.
3 Access the Certificates list on your computer and take a screen shot. Print out a copy.
4 Close Internet Explorer.

→ Practise your skills 3

1 Open a new Word document and enter the rules for setting passwords.
2 Save your document and set a password to modify.
3 Close the document.
4 Re-open the document and use the password to enable you to change some of the text.
5 Close the document.

→ Practise your skills 4

1 Access the Internet and search for software to enable you to lock your computer.
2 Add any useful web sites you find to your Favorites folder.
3 Access one of the bookmarked sites and take a screen shot of the web page.
4 Print out a copy.

→ Check your knowledge 3

1 Which law protects the work of an author or artist?
2 If you had a single-user licence for a software program, could you install it on your friend's computer? Give reasons for your answer.
3 If you were a network administrator in a college with many hundreds of computers to look after, what type of software licence would you need to have the same program available on all the computers?
4 Name one freeware and one shareware program you have used in completing this unit.
5 If you wanted to include a graphic from someone else's web page on your own web site, what would you have to consider?

Practice assignments

Practice assignment 1

For this assignment you will need an e-mail account which can be used for student enquiries. Ask your tutor to set it up for you.

This assignment is broken down into five parts:

1 A brief scenario.
2 Task A requires the candidate to produce information on making a first connection to the Internet and to research viruses.
3 Task B requires the candidate to register for a .Net passport, download and set up a chat program, and research the rules of a chat room.
4 Task C requires the candidate to set up a web-based e-mail account, locate, download and use a compression utility, send an e-mail message with the compressed file as an attachment and set up an automated reply to e-mails.
5 Task D requires the candidate to investigate video/audio conferencing facilities.

You must at all times observe relevant health and safety precautions.

Time allowed: 6 hours

> **Scenario**
> You work as the IT Resource Technician in the Study Centre at Lymegate Further Education College and you are asked to contribute resource materials for the Induction Pack for students joining the college at the start of the academic year. Your responsibility is to provide materials on using the Internet both at home and in the college's Study Centre. You have been set up with an e-mail account which is specifically for student enquiries.

Task A

1 Read the information given in the scenario.
2 Your first task is to provide the information students will need to set up their first Internet connection at home so they will be able to use the college's Virtual Learning Environment.

   Using a suitable search engine, identify the information required and produce a short guide for students. Save your report as CONNECTING.
3 Print out a copy of your report.
4 Using advanced search techniques, locate information about viruses and trojans and the precautions students should take. Take a screen print of your search screen and print out a copy. Label it SCREENPRINT1.
5 Write a bullet list of points to remember about viruses and trojans for the students and save it as VIRUSES. Print out a copy.

6   Go to the Learndirect web site and set this as your homepage. Produce a screen print of your page, print out a copy and label it SCREENPRINT2.

7   On the Learndirect web site find the page which will enable students to register for the newsletter. Copy the URL into a word document and save it as NEWSLETTER.

8   Print out a copy of the document.

Task B

1   Using your Internet connection, locate a site where you can obtain a .Net passport.

2   Register for a .Net passport at the site. Take a screen print showing your successful registration, print out a copy and label it SCREENPRINT3.

3   As an IRC chat program will be used to enable students to contact each other, download and set up a suitable chat program. Take a screen print of the final screen in the setup process, print out a copy and label it SCREENPRINT4.

4   As you want to include some rules on the use of chat facilities, find a suitable chat room and locate the rules. Copy and paste these into a new document and save as CHATRULES. Print out a copy.

5   Select a suitable chat room, one which deals with education if possible. Enter the discussion and take a screen print, print out a copy and label it SCREENPRINT5.

6   Using the information you have gathered, produce a guide to using the program and save it as CHAT.

7   Print out a copy of the guide.

Task C

1   Set up a web-based e-mail account and print out a copy of your registration details. Label it EMAIL.

2   On the Internet, locate a site which will allow the free download of a file compression utility. Download the program and save it to an appropriate location. Take a screen print of the saved location, print out a copy and label it SCREENPRINT6.

3   Using the file compression utility, create an archive and add your documents produced so far. Take a screen print of the archive showing the compressed files, print out a copy and label it SCREENPRINT7.

4   Using your web-based e-mail account send the archive file as an attachment to your enquiries e-mail address.

5   Log on to your enquiries e-mail account and download the compressed file, saving to a suitable location. Take a screen print of the saved file, print out a copy and label it SCREENPRINT8.

6   Set up an automated reply on your enquiries e-mail account to respond to all student enquiries regarding the use of Internet facilities, attaching your archive file. Students are asked to use 'Using the Internet' as the subject header for such enquiries. Print out a copy of your saved message and label it AUTOREPLY.

Task D

1 You are asked to produce a report for the Librarian on using video/audio conferencing as part of a VLE. Using appropriate search techniques locate a program for video/audio conferencing and copy the URL into a new document. Save the document as CONFERENCING.

2 Include in your report CONFERENCING, the possible use of audio/video conferencing, whiteboards, chat and data sharing to support learning.

3 Print out a copy of your document.

Practice assignment 2

For this assignment you will need to work with a partner. Ask your tutor to arrange for a fellow student to complete this exercise with you.

For this assignment you will need an e-mail address which can be used to send an e-mail to your Manager, Clive Small. Ask your tutor to set this up for you.

This assignment is broken down into four parts:

1 A brief scenario.

2 Task A requires the candidate to locate and download an FTP program and to access an etext.

3 Task B requires the candidate to locate and download a conferencing program, and to use the program to exchange information and files.

4 Task C requires the candidate to investigate Internet security and to make changes to browser settings.

You must at all times observe relevant health and safety precautions.

Time allowed: 6 hours

> **Scenario**
> Your job role as IT support at the firm of Texts-To-Go, publishers of etexts, requires you to manage the Internet facilities. Clive Small, the Manager of the company, wants you to find out about the etexts that are currently published on the Internet. Texts-To-Go have offices in three different locations and it is difficult to get all the appropriate staff to a meeting at the head office in London, so Clive would like you to investigate the use of conferencing to facilitate team meetings.
>
> Clive feels that a corporate setting for the browser used by the company would be beneficial and is concerned about the security aspects of using the Internet for business. He has requested a report on these two areas for his consideration.

Task A

1 Read the information given in the scenario.

2 Locate and download an appropriate FTP program. You will need to access your browser settings to ensure that you can download the software you need. Take a screen print of the settings dialogue box showing this. Print out a copy and label it SCREENPRINT1.

3 Clive would like a copy of *Around the World in 80 Days* by Jules Verne and *Origin of the Species*, 6th edition, by Charles Darwin (ask your tutor to allocate one text for you and the other text for your partner in this exercise). Use your FTP program to access a site which publishes etexts, locate the text for this title and download a copy to an appropriate location.

4 Access the etext from the saved location and print out a copy of the first two pages. Label them JULESVERNE or CHARLESDARWIN as appropriate.

5 Enter Clive's e-mail address (which your tutor will give you) into your address book. Take a screen print of your address book, print out a copy and label it SCREENPRINT2.

6 Compose an e-mail to Clive explaining that the etext he requested is attached. Attach the file and send your e-mail. Print out a copy of your e-mail.

Task B

1 Using advanced search tools, investigate the use of conferencing facilities for business purposes and the availability of conferencing software that is free to download. Bookmark sites that you feel are useful. Take a screen print of your Favorites folder. Print out a copy and label it SCREENPRINT3.

2 Using the information you have obtained, prepare a report for Clive on the use of conferencing software for the firm. Make a comment about the conferencing software you would recommend, including your reasons, and explain how you can ensure the software is from a reputable company and will be virus-free. Save the report as CONFERENCING.

3 Print out a copy of the report.

4 Clive has contacted you to say that he accepts your recommendation for conferencing software. Load the appropriate page for the software from your bookmarked sites, print out a copy and label it SOFTWARE. Download and install the program.

5 Work with your colleague to make and receive conference calls using the software. You will need to demonstrate at least three exchanges each. Load the conferencing program and exchange views on your experiences of using the FTP program to obtain the etext. Take a screen print of your discussion, print out a copy and label it SCREENPRINT4.

6 Transfer the etext to your colleague in the conference. Accept the file sent in return and save it to a suitable location. Take a screen print of the saved location, print out a copy and label it SCREENPRINT5.

7 Use the whiteboard facility collaboratively to produce a diagram about your experiences of using conferencing software. Save the file to a suitable location. Print out a copy and label it WHITEBOARD.

8 Open your file CONFERENCING and share it with your colleague. Allow control of the program to enable your colleague to add a point to the document. Save the edited file and print out a copy.

9 Exit the conference call in an appropriate manner and close the program.

Task C

1 Using appropriate search techniques, find information on Internet security features, e.g. virus protection, locks, alerts, digital signatures and passwords. Bookmark any useful sites which detail the use of security locks. Print out a copy of the information obtained, labelling it SECURITY.

2 Using your bookmarks, locate two sites giving details of software which can provide you with the facilities to restrict or enable access to parts of the computer system. Print out a copy of the information and label it LOCKS.

3 Access your browser settings and make changes to:
   a enable images
   b disable sounds
   c disable cookies
   d enable high security restrictions.

   Check your cache settings and note down the value. Take a screen print of the settings dialogue box, print out a copy and label it CACHE.

   Delete all Temporary Internet files on your computer.

4 Add links to the software program you have identified in Task C.2 to your Links bar.

5 Change your browser toolbar settings to give you three different options, e.g. position, turning on or off, appearance, etc. Take screen prints of the three options and print out copies. Label them TOOLBAR1, TOOLBAR2, TOOLBAR3.

6 Decide on the most appropriate option for your company and, using the appropriate screen print, write a report for Clive on the option you have chosen, giving your reasons. Save the report as BROWSER and print out a copy.

Solutions

Section 1 Setting up your connection

Check your knowledge 1 (page 11)

1 A computer, a phone line or cable connection, a modem, an ISP, software – e.g. a web browser, e-mail program, connection software.

2 **a** F **b** T **c** F **d** F **e** T

3 Less than 2 minutes.

4 A specially adapted version of the 56 K modem.

5 Video and audio files. Faster connection means the audio/video will be less jerky and interrupted.

6 Double click on the connected icon on the taskbar.

7 See page 6.

8 A web browser translates the information on the Net into documents that can be viewed on the screen.

9 Small programs developed to handle specific file formats.

10 A browser is used to view web pages, an e-mail program is used to send messages electronically via the Internet.

Check your knowledge 2 (page 38)

1 Your ISP's name, connection type, ISP's phone number, modem details, username, password. To set up your e-mail account you would also need your e-mail address, your ISP's mail server addresses.

2 A higher resolution will mean that you can see more of the web page on your screen.

3 They may load faster.

4 See page 24.

5 See page 26.

6 Four security zones: Internet, Local Intranet, Trusted sites, Restricted sites.

7 Less likely to be able to download files containing a virus.

8 Own answer – see page 28.

9 A web page will load quicker from the cache than having to be loaded from the web site.

10 See page 30.

Section 2 Accessing all areas

Check your knowledge 1 (page 45)

1 HTML (HyperText Markup Language).

2 See page 40.

3 Chat is held in real-time, whereas there is usually a delay between posting to a newsgroup and getting a reply.

4 A special talk program is used for Internet chat.

5 File Transfer Protocol. Used to transfer files across the Internet.

6 FTP

7 See page 44.

8 The images would be clearer and less jerky.

9 Exchange data in real-time.

10 Own answer – see page 44.

Check your knowledge 2 (page 52)

1 See page 46.

2 See page 48.

3 The cursor will change to a hand with a pointing finger.

4 Click the **Home** button on the toolbar.

5 Universal Resource Locator – the Internet address of the web page.

Check your knowledge 3 (page 80)

1 Scan it with an up-to-date virus checker.

2 **Save this program to disk** option.

3 Install it.

4 It has ftp at the beginning of the address rather than http.

5 Chat is held in real-time, whereas there is usually a delay between posting to a newsgroup and getting a reply.

6 It would be viewed as shouting.

7 A special talk program is used for Internet chat.

8 Internet Relay Chat.

9 No one controls the Internet.

10 Own answer – see page 74 on.

Section 3 Electronic mail

Check your knowledge 1 (page 102)

1 To enable you to access your e-mail messages when away from your home or work.

2 See page 83.

3 To enable you to check for new messages on both accounts at the same time.

4 To respond to messages when you are away from your computer to let the senders know their messages have been received.

5 See page 93.

6 Home address, phone number, business details, birthdays, anniversaries, etc.

7 Select the contact's name in the address book and press the **Delete** key.

8 So that you can send the same e-mail message to all the contacts in your group without having to enter the addresses individually.

9 By selecting the appropriate option from the **View/Sort by** menu.

10 See page 101.

Section 4 Internet conferencing

Check your knowledge 1 (page 121)

1 A computer with a connection to the Internet, a sound card, speakers and microphone, video camera or web cam, conferencing program, fast connection to the Internet for audio/video.

2 See page 103.

3 Chat, voice, video, whiteboard, file transfer, data sharing, program sharing, desktop sharing.

4 To collaboratively discuss, edit or produce an agreed drawing/plan, etc.

5 Any

6 You can share a running program, even if it isn't installed on all the participants' computers.

7 A fast Internet connection, good video/audio equipment.

8 MCU (multipoint control units) allow multipoint conferencing, or communication between more than two parties at once.

9 Own answer – see page 118.

10 See page 119 on.

Section 5 Safe surfing

Check your knowledge 1 (page 130)

1 No. Viruses and trojans, physical theft of the computer, colleagues at work, are all threats to the security of data, etc.

2 See page 125.

3 Up-date it by logging on to the provider's web site.

4 A broadband connection is 'always on' and therefore provides more opportunities for an attack.

5 Firewalls prevent unauthorised access to your computer by monitoring all activity.

6 Symmetric key and public key (asymmetric) encryption.

7 From a certificate authority's web site.

8 The address would be shown as https, rather than the usual http.

9 Encrypting e-mail messages will ensure they remain private.

10 Your public key.

Check your knowledge 2 (page 143)

1 A public key, a private key and a digital signature.

2 By the red rosette against their details in the address book.

3 See page 131.

4 See page 134.

5 See page 137 on.

6 This would be too easy for someone to guess. She would need a password made up of letters and numbers, or something similar, that would be hard to guess.

7 Own answer.

8 Own answer.

9 To allow or restrict rights to certain parts or functions of the network.

10 An audible or visual alarm that signals an error, represents a warning of some sort, or informs you of an event.

Check your knowledge 3 (page 145)

1 The Copyright Design and Patents Act 1988.

2 No, it is only for use on one machine at a time.

3 Site licence as it allows all users within a site to use the program.

4 Own answer.

5 If you use any images from other people you could be infringing copyright law if you don't seek permission or check with the small print that it is OK to do so.

Glossary

ADSL	Asymmetric Digital Subscriber Line. A technology using high frequencies in standard telephone lines in order to transmit data.
Attachment	A file which is sent along with an e-mail message.
Bookmark	Also called **Favorite** in Internet Explorer. A list of frequently visited, marked sites to enable one click access.
Bps	Bits per second. The unit of measurement for the speed of data transmission over the Internet.
Browser	The program that allows you to view web pages on the Internet.
Bug	A faulty piece of coding in a computer program.
Cache	A copy of the pages visited on the Web stored on an area of your hard drive called the cache.
Chat	'Rooms' on the Internet where you can have live, online conversations.
Compression	Software which is used to reduce the size of a file.
Connection	Connecting a computer to the Internet, usually through an ISP.
Cookies	Information stored as a text file on your computer from web sites you have visited.
Cracker	A person who cracks the code in software to copy or misuse it illegally.
Directories	Listing of web sites classified into subject areas.
Domain	Part of the name for an Internet computer that tells other computers where it is and the type of organisation that owns it.
Download	Obtaining a file from a web site usually by clicking on a word or icon on the page.
E-commerce	Buying and selling products and services online
E-mail	Electronic mail. A way of sending messages from one computer to another across a network.
Encryption	Files that have been coded that can't be read without a special key.
FAQ	Frequently Asked Questions. A list of the most common questions, often asked by newcomers to using Internet services, together with the answers.
Favorite	Also called **Bookmark**. A list of frequently visited, marked sites to enable one click access.
Firewall	Software or hardware which monitors traffic between computer and Internet to prevent unauthorised access.
Freeware	Software that is free to use.
FTP	File Transfer Protocol. The system used to transfer files from one computer to another.
Hacker	Someone who gains unauthorised access to a computer to look at, change or destroy data.
History	A record of the URLs you have visited stored in a list by your browser.
Hit	A web page found by a search engine in response to keywords entered in a search box.
Homepage	The front page of a web site, or the opening page in your browser.
HTML	HyperText Markup Language. The language used to write web pages.
HTTP	HyperText Transfer Protocol. The system used to transfer web pages over the Internet.
Hyperlink	Used to jump from one web page to another. Hyperlinks can be images or underlined text.
Inbox	The folder where incoming messages are placed.
Internet	The network of interconnected computers that communicate using special protocols.
IP	Internet Protocol. The system used to specify how data is transferred over the Internet.
IP Address	The unique number which identifies each computer on the Internet.
IRC	Internet Relay Chat. Internet chat using specific programs.
ISDN	Integrated Services Digital Network. A high-speed telephone connection which can transfer data over the Internet very quickly.
ISP	Internet Service Provider. Companies which provide a gateway to the Internet.
Keyword	A word that represents a document's contents.
Link	A connection between two computers. Highlighted text or images which connect web pages.
Mailbox	The place where e-mail is kept on an ISP server.

MIME	Multipurpose Internet Mail Extension. The system used to include non-text information, such as attached files, in an e-mail message.
Modem	Equipment to translate analogue signals to digital signals, and vice versa, to enable computers to transmit data.
Netiquette	Informal rules about the way to behave on the Internet.
Network	Computers linked together to share information and services.
Newsgroups	An Internet discussion forum. The discussions are not held in real-time.
Offline	Not connected to the Internet.
Online	Connected to the Internet.
Online Services	Company that provides access to its own network as well as to the Internet.
Outbox	The folder where outgoing messages are placed.
Page	A document or information available on the Internet.
Plug-ins	Features added to the browsers to give extra functionality, such as playing music, reading special text formats.
POP	Point of Presence. A point of access to the Internet.
POP 3	Post Office Protocol – the protocol used to receive messages
Protocol	A set of rules used by computers to communicate with each other.
Search engines	An online service that will search web pages for keywords entered in a search box.
Shareware	Software which you can try before you buy.
SMTP	Simple Mail Transfer Protocol – the protocol used to send messages.
Snail mail	Mail delivered by the normal postal system.
TCP/IP	The language computers on the Internet use to communicate with each other.
Thread	The progress of a discussion in a forum as replies are posted.
Trojan	A program which, once on your computer, will allow a hacker to gain access to your data and programs.
Upload	To copy a file from your computer to another computer via the Internet.
URL	Universal Resource Locator. The address given to all the different resources on the Internet.
Usenet	A network of computers that host forums.
Virus	A destructive program hidden in other files and programs that can damage files on your hard drive.
Web page	A document written in HTML and linked to other documents by hyperlinks. Shown as a single screen in your browser.
Web site	A collection of web pages set up by an organisation or individual.
World Wide Web	The friendly face of the Internet. Formatted text and graphics which make up pages on the Internet.
Worm	A program that can reproduce itself on a computer and eventually use up all the computer's resources.